BOOK
PUBLISHING
SECRETS
FOR ENTREPRENEURS

JOHN NORTH

#1 International Best Seller

BOOK PUBLISHING SECRETS
FOR ENTREPRENEURS

How to Create an International Best - Selling Book in as Little as 90 Days Without Writing a Single Word!

WRITTEN BY JOHN NORTH

5 Time #1 International Best Selling Author

EDITED BY JAMES NORTH

Grab your FREE "Secret Publishing Kit" from
www.evolveglobalpublishing.com/spk

Book Publishing Secrets for Entrepreneurs:
How to Create an International Best - Selling Book in as Little as 90 Days Without Writing a Single Word!

1st Edition. 2019

ASIN: B07NJ9G9VC (Amazon Kindle)
ISBN: 978-1-09131-369-9 (Amazon Print)
ISBN: 978-1-68454-422-6 (Ingram Spark) PAPERBACK
ISBN: 978-1-68454-423-3 (Ingram Spark) HARDCOVER
ISBN: (Smashwords)

CONTACT THE AUTHOR:

Business Name: EVOLVE SYSTEMS GROUP PTY LTD
Author Website: www.johnnorth.com.au
Main Website: www.EvolveGlobalPublishing.com
LinkedIn: https://au.linkedin.com/in/johnnorth1085
Twitter: @johnnorth7 and @evolveauthor
Book Bonus: www.evolveinstantauthor.com
Email: john@evolvesys.com.au
Phone: 1300 889 383

TABLE OF CONTENTS

ABOUT THE AUTHOR

Five-Time #1 International Best Selling Author, John North is a versatile and experienced entrepreneur with a solid background in Accounting, Banking, Finance, Personal Development, IT, Marketing and Business Management.

John has Five #1 Best Selling Books about publishing, business strategy and internet marketing and his passion for Squash.

John currently holds a number of titles, including CEO of Evolve Systems Group, Associate Diploma in Business (Accounting) and Fellow of the Institute of Public Accountants.

John's passion is to help business owners become more strategic and smarter about their marketing efforts. He constantly pushes the envelope of what's possible in this modern era and is widely regarded among his peers as very innovative and highly creative in his approach.

In the digital era of the business world, internet marketing is the ruling king. Not only does it broaden your company's reach and ensure your brand's visibility, but it can also generate prospects and even turn them into loyal customers.

John has created Evolve Global Publishing as a premier service to enable him to help thousands rather than hundreds of entrepreneurs. He believes anyone can follow a system to success, but the missing keys are implementation and accountability. Evolve Global Publishing's platform and methodologies allow an entrepreneur and potential author to create and publish their own book in a little as 90 days without writing a single word!

ABOUT EVOLVE GLOBAL PUBLISHING

www.evolveglobalpublishing.com.au

Evolve Global Publishing has been responsible for publishing hundreds of books and all of them, **without fail, have achieved #1 best-seller status on Amazon.**

Evolve Global Publishing offers a worry-free professional service to achieve the creation, publishing, and launch of your book.

We are about to introduce you to the **"Single Most Powerful Tool to Promote and Market Your Business"**

- The solution is 564 years old.
- It's not high-tech.
- It's won the hearts and minds of people all over the world.
- It can create wealth and fame for those who understand its power.
- It works in any business or industry, in any language, anywhere in the world.

Published authors **make more money**, get more attention, have more freedom, and are given the opportunity to share their message with the world.

Research has also shown that entrepreneurs who have written books have a distinct advantage. According to a BusinessWeek survey, 96% of authors saw positive benefits from their book, such as easier access to media/PR exposure, the command of higher speaking and consulting fees, an increase in their credibility and reach—and simply more income.

IMAGINE ...

You can create a nonfiction book and become a bestseller while attracting a steady flow of new business.

You're connected to the biggest names in your industry, capitalising on your star power to promote your products and services.

You create a growing tribe on Facebook, LinkedIn, YouTube, Google+, and iTunes, and receive lots of new business from all this exposure.

You become recognized as an authority—even a celebrity in your field—in a few months, *not* years or decades.

You attract people who want to join you and help you and your business, life, and mission because your vision inspires and move them to action.

The biggest brands, platforms, and networks in the world like Google, YouTube, Amazon, Twitter, Apple, Instagram, LinkedIn, and Facebook, etc., will help promote and sell your books, build your list and reputation, all while promoting your content to social networks.

Evolve Global Publishing's normal publishing process includes:

1. Creation of your content either from your existing assets or through a series of recorded interviews
2. Book cover and title—creation/design or use your existing files
3. Formatting of your manuscript for print and digital formats, including softcover and hardcover
4. Number one best-seller campaign in multiple categories
5. Publishing for digital and print for Amazon, CreateSpace, Apple, and Kobo
6. Arrangement of physical printed books (additional print cost)
7. Optional editing and proofreading services

Publishing Solutions

Once your book is ready for worldwide release, Evolve Global Publishing will enable your book to be purchased on virtually every known platform. We will make your book available to thousands of major online and offline bookstores and retailers, which expands the size of the potential audience for your books.

#1 International Best-Seller Campaign

As part of your membership package, we will execute our #1 international best-seller strategy designed to have you listed as, at the least, #1 best-seller, with a goal for #1 in three Amazon categories in four countries (one per country).

We will continue to promote your book until we achieve this goal. Because achieving #1 best-seller status requires significant marketing and promotion on our side, we charge an additional fee.

GET IT ALL DONE IN AS LITTLE AS 90 DAYS

Our goal is to assist you to create your content and publish it within a 90-day period. However, these timescales can vary depending on individual requirements. But it's about getting you out there fast! The ones that invest in this system will change their lives and businesses forever.

THE QUESTION IS—ARE YOU SIMPLY INTERESTED? OR *ARE YOU COMMITTED?*

Are you *committed* to getting the additional freedom a book will give you, being in an elite group of published authors, and getting recognized and standing out?

We look forward to making you our next best-selling author!

Book an obligation-free call at www.evolveglobalpublishing. com, and let's get you started!

INTRODUCTION

We speak to many entrepreneurs every day, and this question eventually comes up …

"What's the fastest and easiest way to boost my marketing and get more customers?"

Almost without exception, we answer, *"A book"*.

You can base your book around your business, or you can use it to start a whole new business.

The great thing about writing a book is that it not only ensures that you get crystal clear on what you do, but also on how you do it.

However, it's very common for self-doubt to set in after the initial enthusiasm. Numerous unhelpful thoughts chatter away at the forefront of your mind. First and foremost—*"I'm not a writer"*.

To that, we say, *"Authors are always better-paid than writers!"*

You can hire editors or writers to help you create your book and your vision. Having a clear vision and idea of what you want your book to be and do for the reader is far more important than being a great writer.

Another worry—*"I don't have a spare year to go into the mountains and write a book!"*

What if we said you can create a book in as little as 90 days without ever actually writing a single word?

This book is a complete guide on how to create and publish your very own book in 90 days or less.

What stops a lot of authors in their tracks is seemingly unavoidable bottlenecks, like spending weeks finding a publisher, or another week re-editing your manuscript for a publisher to accept your submission, or spending an entire month just on finding the right cover for your book.

The truth is, all of these time-sinks can be avoided, side-stepped, or accelerated greatly.

But this book is about more than just using your time wisely. We have also provided a significant amount of advice and directions on how to produce valuable content and refine it, how to create a beautifully designed cover for your book in a short period of time, how to get your book published across numerous popular platforms quickly, how to make the existence of your book known to your target audience, and most importantly, how to make your book work for you—not the other way around. To that end, it's important to understand the current climate that you're attempting to get your book published in.

The book publishing industry has been dramatically redefined since Amazon changed the way we find and consume books. They have put extreme pressure on the traditional book publisher to compete with Amazon's all-in-one distribution and marketplace system.

How can you compete with a company that is available to everyone, internationally, 24/7, with lower price points than anybody else, prime delivery within two hours, an endless supply of stock because third-party sellers eagerly take over distribution and fulfilment for no cost, and an offering of literally millions of unique items (especially those obscure books you won't find in your local Barnes & Noble easily) for sale beyond just books? That's the exact same question traditional book publishers have been forced to ask themselves in the Age of Amazon.

Amazon alone has millions of books available to purchase with one click, and all of the books you've ever bought are ready to read, right there on your mobile device or computer. There is a common misconception that physical books are slowly going out of fashion. But the reality is that it's the way we buy books that have changed.

Bookstores struggle to compete with the likes of Amazon, but the actual printing of books has increased. Even Amazon, a company that has more heavily embraced the digital revolution than any other company in the business, continues to expand their print facilities to keep up with demand.

Physical books aren't going out of fashion. Physical bookstores are.

And because bookstores have gone digital, now is the best time to write your own book! It's easier than ever to get your book on the biggest bookstores on the web.

You may be wondering why you should publish your own book. It's astonishing how many doors open just because you have a book.

When you publish your book, it's there forever. It leaves a legacy behind for your family to remember you by and learn about you from, even generations later. Even if there are three million books on Amazon, there are over seven billion people on the planet alive today. That's a very small percentage of authors compared to the general population.

Also, did you know that the word "author" is actually short for "AUTHORITY"?

If you want to dominate your industry, write a book to show everyone you are an AUTHORITY. We're not talking about a massive book here, either. An average-length book at 30,000 to 40,000 words will be around 150 to 180 pages. That's a nice-sized book. It's economic to print and deliver, and easy to carry a few on the plane or to meetings.

Imagine showing up to your next sales meeting and handing a personally-signed book to your prospect. It's a powerful message to send to a potential customer looking for someone who knows what they're talking about. The conversation generally moves to how much and when you can do the job, rather than whether you are qualified to help them. After all, you just handed them 150 pages worth of reasons why you are the right person for the job.

Creating and publishing a book is a journey of discovery that will benefit you for years to come. In the Age of Amazon, digital distribution, and print on demand, getting your book out to your target audience has never been easier. If you have a computer, a word processor, and an internet connection, you have everything you absolutely need to publish a book.

However, even in today's modern, digital world, getting a book published is still a tricky task. There are pitfalls and time-wasters everywhere, and many things that authors don't even consider when writing their books ambush them out of left field, months later. You can lose thousands of dollars by making the wrong choices and in some cases, give up because it gets too hard or expensive to finish it.

The five core secrets to book publishing have guided every chapter of this book to completion. They will save you countless hours of your time and help you evolve your book to the next level!

evolveglobalpublishing.com

BECOME AN AUTHOR TODAY.

CONCEIVE IT, CREATE IT, AND PUBLISH IT IN LESS THAN 90 DAYS!

We are about to reveal to you the five core secrets to publishing your own best-selling book that we would normally charge thousands of dollars to access.

Our systems and methodologies have been developed and tested through helping hundreds of entrepreneurs become best-selling authors in a matter of months, not years.

Far too many aspiring authors don't plan ahead and end up having to confront roadblock after roadblock, stumbling their way through their industry with no clear goalposts or any indication that they are headed in the right direction, up until they finally publish their book. Writing, publishing, and promoting a book is a convoluted process, full of unforgiving traps and tricks that seem to crop up without warning. Many authors write several books before they really figure out what they're doing.

You don't have to struggle the way so many writers do. This book aims to demystify the book publishing process and provide you with the knowledge and tools you need to get your book into the hands of as many people as possible. But more than that, it's about how you can make your book work for you.

The secrets are here for you to discover, but you need to find them, and the only way to do that is to turn the page.

WHY SHOULD YOU CREATE A BOOK?

We spoke to you briefly in the introduction about how a book is a fast way to create more leads and sales in your business. We want to now dig deeper into the first secret of book publishing.

Believe it or not many authors don't actually consider the true reason for writing their book. It's vitally important to know what outcome you want for your book, especially your first one!

ESTABLISH AUTHORITY

A book is an instant expert authority booster for you and your business, which will p osition your authority. In your book you can demonstrate your genius, knowledge, wisdom, and experience.

GET MORE SALES AND PROSPECTS

Published authors make money and help more people. Becoming an author also allows you to g enerate multiple income streams.

Books allow you to sell your products and services faster and easier. Books can also talk about what you do, who you do it for, including case studies and results, and invite the reader to try out your products and services.

Before we get into the strategies you can employ in your business, we want to discuss a little shortcut. Everyone has someone in their industry that stands out; someone who seems to be the expert. How did they end up being considered a leader?

Often, because of social proof. They have given their peers enough evidence to indicate that they must be an expert.

Whatever business you're in, your #1 priority will always be to get new clients. But with all these distractions, how do you find the time?

What if we told you that there is a 100% guaranteed way to land new clients, as well as upsell new products, get yourself lucrative speaking gigs, and much more? And what if this solution made you a household name in your field? The go-to expert for advice and information among all your clients and even the media?

It's more than possible—and you can start right away. The solution is simply to write a book. There can be no better lead generator, foot-in-the-door solution, and media promotional tool. Suddenly, you'll be inundated with new business and become known as the expert in your field. And it's much easier than you might think.

First, let's look in detail at exactly what a book can do for you and your business. Then, later on, we'll describe how easy it is to write such a book.

A book boosts your credibility.

A book, or rather, your book, will position you and your business at the highest level. Think of how much marketing clout you'll have when you can add "#1 best-selling author" to your name, including in business correspondence—right down to your email signature. You can even hand out your book in place of a business card, as well as in meetings. This is a badge of respect that shows you're an authority on the subject of your book and have the experience to back it up.

A book opens doors—literally!

Have you ever had the frustrating experience of not being able to reach the decision-maker in an organisation?

Perhaps you need to meet the CEO of a company you want to do business with, but you are only getting as far as their secretary who always fobs you off. Now imagine sending them your book, gift-wrapped, with a hand-written note to contact you, the book's author.

These people will have already "met" you in your book, so getting in touch with them will be that much easier. In fact, they may very well contact you first.

A book generates leads and builds customer databases.

Believe it or not, a book can be one of the most cost-effective ways of building loyalty and getting new leads and new business. Each sentence, paragraph, and chapter can be a call to action to the reader. It doesn't even need to be a hard sell at this point. You can give away free reports, free trials, free consultations ... the list is almost endless, and it all helps in getting you nearer to closing a deal or winning a new customer.

Do it smartly and you'll capture the reader's email address and other details to add to your database. Consider this also: for every ten books you sell on Amazon, you will likely get contact details for two to four leads, meaning you are getting paid for the sale of the books, *and* getting qualified leads. What a bargain!

A book can act as a marketing tool for your specific area of expertise.

Your book can include examples of what you or your business does, so that readers will understand your business better. These can be in the form of lessons, how-to guides, demonstrations and other hands-on and practical information that will ensure readers are engaged with your business, understand your expertise, and trust that you're the right match for them.

Writing a best-selling book is a way to win professional attention.

If you're a businessperson, you'll know the value of getting speaking gigs and other high-profile jobs, both to establish yourself as a professional and an authority in your field and to promote your products and services. You may even have tried before to get in front of a professional audience to promote yourself or your product, but have been frustrated because the professional body won't take you seriously. So, imagine introducing yourself as the author of a #1 best-selling book and observe the response. In all likelihood, professional organisations and event managers will be queuing up to have you speak at their events.

A book will garner media attention.

Each chapter or section of your book—any part of it, in fact—can be used for promotional purposes in the media. You can send commentators and pundits your book along with your contact details. Inevitably, you'll get invitations to be on talk shows and other media vehicles. Pundits will know what questions to ask you because they've read your book—and you, being the expert that you are, will know how to reply because it's in your book! You can also use chapters, themes and sections of your book to generate social media posts or tweets. You can make these as hands-on as you like, the goal being to keep people aware of you, your book and your business.

Books build local businesses.

A common misconception is that only huge multinational corporations or international companies have books. This simply isn't true. Whether you're a big or small company, global or local, having a best-selling book to your name always puts you ahead of the competition. Imagine handing out copies of your book to potential clients in your local area. This says far more about your professionalism than the photocopied flyers that your closest competitor uses.

Marketing in regulated businesses is easy.

Certain business areas like finance, stocks and share trading, law and healthcare are heavily-regulated, which puts people off when it comes to writing in these fields.

It shouldn't, because no one can prevent you from writing about personal experiences and from giving personal advice. Just because an industry is regulated doesn't rule you out from writing a book about it.

You will make more money. Simple as that.

Books make people money for all the reasons outlined above. It's all about joining an elite group of people; "a members only club" who rise above the rest because they've had the confidence and commitment to write one or more books. Your partners will be companies like Amazon and Apple, who will assist you in selling and marketing your book on their own sites or on social media. It's like being on a roller coaster of success that never stops.

But writing a book takes time, and you need to be a professional writer, right?

Wrong. There are actually three myths to debunk here.

MYTH #1

The first is believing that you need to be a professional or experienced "author" to write a book. This is one of the biggest hurdles to the practicalities of writing a book. In fact, anyone can write a book, especially a business professional with something to say.

MYTH #2

The second is the belief that you have to be super smart to write a book. In fact, most authors are not geniuses—they simply got their hands dirty and set to work writing about what they know. Some will, of course, have used a professional editor to help organize their ideas or tidy up their grammar.

MYTH #3

The third is that you have to be rich or famous to write a book, which is plain nonsense. Look at J.K. Rowling, author of the Harry Potter books. When she started out, she was barely making a living. Now she's one of the wealthiest authors alive today.

So where do you go from here?

At Evolve Global Publishing, we have a simple 5-Step system which is designed for small business owners, entrepreneurs, speakers, consultants, coaches and professionals just like you. This will help you to create your book and become recognised as the go-to expert, authority and star in your field. It overcomes the three myths mentioned above that all budding authors have to face.

The system is based on five steps, specifically:

- **Designing**—mainly strategy around your book including the customer journey
- **Creating**—the fast-track method to writing your book
- **Publishing**—the formatting and publish process
- **Promoting**—time to launch your book to the world!
- **Evolving**—what now?

So, How Do You Start?

Our innovative system can take you from scratch to the top-10 best-seller lists in ninety days or less. It's so easy, it's no wonder our client list keeps growing.

And here's why: you don't have to write a single word! In most cases, all we need is ten to fifteen hours of your time to record your content, after which it will then be transcribed to text. Next you'll work with one of our experienced editors to complete the final version.

You know that you need to write a book. I hope we've convinced you of this fact. Or maybe you're an existing author whose book didn't perform well the first time. This is where we step in. Evolve Global Publishing offers packages designed for everyone, from complete beginners to seasoned authors.

Remember you are an author, not a writer!

Here are some great reasons to write a book ...

Reason #1: Credibility

- A book is an instant credibility booster for you and your business.
- It supplies you with positioning and authority.
- In your book, you can demonstrate your genius, knowledge, wisdom, and experience.

Reason #2: Exposure to New Clients

- A book is the ultimate foot-in-the-door strategy.

Reason #3: Lead-Generating

- You can use your book to get traffic, leads and build your contact database.
- A book is a library full of social proof, examples, stories and ways to show you care, that you know what you're

talking about, and that you can help the reader to solve just about any challenge.

Reason #4: Showcasing You

- Books can be used to sell your services and products faster and easier.
- They can also talk about what you do, who you do it for, provide case studies and results, and invite the reader to try you out.

Reason #5: Creating New Roles

- Books can be used to create new positions for yourself or your client as a consultant.

Reason #6: Speaking Opportunities

- Writing books is a great way to get or increase your speaking opportunities.

Reason #7: Media Opportunities and Marketing

- Having a book is the perfect way to get media attention including radio shows, TV interviews, and creating attention on social media.
- A book can provide a roadmap for your messaging and marketing.

Reason #8: Building Local Business

- A book can be used to build your business locally.

Reason #9: Great for Regulated Industries

- Regulated industries include fields like financial planning, investing, medical, healthcare, etc.

- Even though they are regulated, this is not normally a barrier to having a book, and can be a great way of marketing in heavily-regulated industries.

Reason #10: Wealth and Wellbeing Accelerant

- Published authors make money and help more people.

WHAT KIND OF BOOK SHOULD YOU CREATE?

Every author we have worked with has had an idea on what their book should be about. Many ideas, in fact. If anything, they have had too many ideas in mind for just one book.

But often they don't think about the kind of book they want to create. Neither do they think about how they want to position themselves based on the book they want to write.

They know that they want to be known as an author and an expert in their field. What they don't think about is how this desired outcome should impact the type of book they should be creating. Unfortunately it's common to end up with a book half-finished before realising that you're writing for the wrong audience, or you're shooting yourself in the foot by providing the wrong type or amount of content.

Let's say you are an entrepreneur that wants to position yourself as a marketing expert that readers should come to if they want marketing done for them. It's common for an author in this situation to write in full detail about how they do their own marketing. While this shows the reader that you are knowledgeable in your field, it's not necessarily going to attract the right prospect for your business.

If you focused more on the "what" and the "why", with just some of the "how", this would become the perfect book to attract a prospect that is more likely to be prepared to pay for your services.

A great reference source for this type of book is *The E-Myth Revisited* by Michael E Gerber. In our opinion, this is the best lead generator book ever written. The first half of the book is about a business owner and her journey. Gerber describes a painful story to get the reader emotionally invested, also allowing them to see themselves in the same situation. The latter half of the book gives the reader some solid ideas on how to implement change in their own business. It gives them just enough information to be able to get some instant wins, but leaves them wanting more and a desire to contact the writer for more help.

Conversely, let's say you're a marketing expert that writes a book about your legacy discussing all the successes and failures that you experienced during your 20 years on the job. For example, you could talk about why small businesses won't benefit from investing huge amounts of money on marketing when they should be more focused on positioning themselves correctly to attract the right customers. This would be more of a do-it-yourself style book, and it will be harder to get the reader to want your help.

So, the first question to ask yourself is, what type of book do you want to write?

Do you want to write a **legacy book**, one that focuses on you and what you've done? Or do you want to write a **logic book**, one that focuses on what your business has done, how your business does it, and how your business can help an eager reader?

Before you begin your book you need to consider:

- Should you be writing exhaustively about your most successful process as a business and describing in detail how every intricate step works?
- Should you be covering your business and processes in just enough detail that a reader, unfamiliar with the industry, can get a good handle on the importance your business and industry?
- Are you writing a textbook or a practical hands-on style book?

- Do you want your readers to take your process and implement it into their business, or do you want them to want you to implement it for them?

Establish your end goals at the outset, and base the thrust and content of your book around it.

One of the best questions to ask yourself is what you shouldn't put in your book. For example, as a heart surgeon, you might want to educate a reader on heart disease, how the heart works, and the best lifestyle choices, but you wouldn't want to teach them how to do their own heart surgery! This example is a bit extreme, but it makes a good point for any book that is designed to take the reader from being unconvinced about your topic to better informed and a true believer in your abilities.

Make sure you are very clear about the goals of your book. In some cases, it's a good idea to write the last chapter, or at least the last couple of pages, before you write the rest of the book. This will give you an endpoint to work towards.

Our Simple 5-Step System

Almost everyone has wanted to write a book at some point in their life–they may have even tried writing it, only to give up not long after. Whether they wanted to write a fiction or non-fiction book, they stopped writing it because they felt like they weren't making any progress. Perhaps it was just a big mess with no underlying idea or structure holding it together, or maybe they were stuck staring at the chapter title, hoping a perfect string of words would somehow inspire themselves into existence.

All of these roadblocks are caused by confusion about what their book should be, what they should be writing about, or how to tie a myriad of disparate paragraphs and chapters into one whole–a book.

Unfortunately, wanting to write a book, and even knowing what you want to write about, is not enough to actually complete a book. You have to know where you're going and you need to follow some kind of logical system that ensures you will be able to finish your book. Something that you can refer to whenever you feel you're losing your way.

Fortunately, this book is precisely about following that sort of system, a system designed to quickly and simply produce the book that you or your business needs. You don't necessarily have to follow this system, although it has been tested and refined by hundreds of clients who *have* finished and published their own books, but you should follow *a* system. If you don't, you'll fall off the track, and end up wasting a lot of valuable time trying to figure out how to get everything back on track.

We used our own 5-step system in order to write the book you're reading at this very moment. We're not leaving out details or claiming willful ignorance on certain elements of the process. This is the exact process, step-by-step, that we used to write *Book Publishing Secrets for Entrepreneurs*. This is a short summary of what we'll be asking you to do in order to finish your book.

If you feel like a certain element of the process is unnecessary or could be handled differently, remember that you don't have to follow this system religiously. It's your book, not ours. However, try to understand why we ask you to do certain things, and not do others. Deviating from the steps we detail in *Book Publishing Secrets for Entrepreneurs*, especially early on, is likely to cause trouble later on. If you feel you have a good reason to ignore a step or change it slightly, just be aware that this system works best the less you stray from this tried-and-true success path.

STEP 1: DESIGNING YOUR BOOK

The first question you must ask yourself is, "Why should I write a book?" It's our belief that every person has at least 120 pages of content in them that they need to get out to the world. Being able to say that you've written a book, and being able to put a copy of it in a prospective client's hands is a very valuable thing.

Just because you've written a book about the field that you are trying to sell your services in, people will look to you as an expert. Your credibility will skyrocket simply because you have a book and you will be able to generate business leads from people who have read your book because they respect you as an expert.

But before you write anything, we need to lay the groundwork. This means thinking about who you are writing your book for and why it should matter to them, what kind of ideas you want to push, and whether you want to write your book to carry your legacy or to generate leads. If it's the former, the content of your book will be framed in a very different way than if you want it to be a lead generator.

After we have all of those important details and concepts mapped out, we need to work out a title, a cover, and a table of contents (i.e., the subjects and ideas you want to cover throughout your book). We discuss creating a marketable title and an eye-catching cover in detail because these are the very first things a prospective reader will see. The table of contents is the next thing they will see, which is why you need to organise your book correctly and include several key topics you think your target audience will be interested in.

As an experienced publisher, we have been able to streamline the process from conception to publication so as to be able to produce a high-quality book in the shortest timeframe possible. Within 90 days, we have gotten numerous author's books written, published, and to #1 international best-seller status. This book shares many of the secrets that make this possible.

STEP 2: CREATING YOUR BOOK

Now that you know who you're writing your book for and what you're writing about, we need to get it written. But first, there are a few things you need to keep in mind while you are creating your book, as they will have an impact on later steps in the process. The first part of this process is to utilise various unique methods of rapid content creation in order to get the bulk of your words onto the pages so that you can later refine and rework it. Performing your content, telling stories, or interviewing another expert are some of the most effective ways you can build more content into the book quickly.

If you've done the previous step correctly, most of the work left will be in organising and refining your content. All books need at least one proofread, and possibly some editing, to make sure that the writing is of the highest quality possible.

STEP 3: PUBLISHING YOUR BOOK

Gone are the days when you have to shop your book around to publisher after publisher in an effort to find someone who will print your book and get it on store shelves. In the digital era, self-publishing a book has never been easier.

Huge companies like Amazon, Apple, and Google want your book on their site so they can market it to their customer base and make money. Aside from big online publishers, there are also many smaller ones, like BookBaby and Smashwords.

Of them all, Amazon is the single biggest and widest-reaching book publisher, and it's likely where you'll likely get most of your mileage. They will publish your book not only in eBook format, but also offer you the option to print it in paperback.

Part of this publishing process also requires that you get all of your files and related information organised—mostly by yourself. Many of these publishers offer you a platform to publish your book, but you will need to provide them with several files and information, such as an ISBN, the book's content, and a cover. Your content and cover will need to be provided in the correct file format, which is typically PDF format.

There are several speed bumps and snags you may hit on the way to publishing your book, so it is important that the publishing process is undertaken as rigorously as possible. Your cover may not print correctly, or words might be cut off or formatted strangely, and these things are likelier to happen when you are dealing with multiple formats, such as eBook, paperback, and hardcover.

Ideally, however, you want to publish your book in as many formats as possible to make it as available as possible to readers. If you only have an eBook published on Amazon, many readers won't regard it as nearly as authentically as they view paperback books.

Publishing your book as an audiobook is another great option that is far more difficult than the rest, so it is best done after you have already been published in the traditional formats. Even still, having an audiobook version of your book is one of the best things you can do to raise your credibility and the authenticity of your book in the eyes of readers.

STEP 4: PROMOTING YOUR BOOK

Promoting your book is the step that most authors fail to do correctly. This is largely because authors aren't willing to promote it. Many creative people seem to have the notion, "If it's good, people will come", but the truth is that if you don't promote it, nobody is ever going to know about it. This applies to all creative endeavours.

Another common mistake that creative people make is refusing to vouch for the quality of their work. It's a case of taking creative integrity too far, saying, "The work should speak for itself", and being unwilling to promote it or even speak well of it. It's a weird sense of shame that comes over every proud creator.

The truth is, there is nothing to be ashamed about. If you think your hard work has resulted in something respectable, say as much. Why would anyone want to read a book that you can't even say out loud is worth reading?

Plug your book. Speak well of it. Recommend it to people you think will benefit from reading it. There is no shame in rallying for something you believe in, even if that something is your own work. Embrace your pride in your creation.

And now that you're actually willing to promote your book, there are several great ways of doing so. The very first thing you should do is run a best-seller campaign and get your book to #1. This will do more to grab eyes than anything else. It's the ultimate credibility booster. After you've done this, it's a great springboard for being able to take your book around to podcasts, social media, the radio, and perhaps even television to talk about your book.

The best thing you can do to generate interest in your book is to talk about it. Talk about who it's for, what they'll get from it, and why you wrote it for them.

STEP 5:
EVOLVING
YOUR BOOK

A lot of authors view their book as both the starting point and the endpoint. They don't think much further than the book. They don't think about how they can leverage their book to retain a captive audience or funnel them into another program (or, in the case of professional writers, funnel readers into another book).

Not using your book to accomplish something is untapped potential. Your book is a tool. But you have to use it correctly and intelligently, or you won't get the results you want.

First, you need to figure out what you want to use your book for. This could be any number of things:

- Creating a community
- Funneling interested readers into another product or program
- Establishing a reputation as an authority

We will go through some of the best ways you can use your book to grow your business, create an audience, build your reputation, and more. These are strategies that have worked for us and for hundreds of our authors.

Evolving your book is about creating a relationship between you and your reader, and capitalising on that connection in order to achieve your desired outcome. A book is a powerful tool and resource—if you use it well.

WE CAN
HELP CREATE
YOUR BOOK

While we've attempted to simplify and expedite the process as much as possible, these steps are involved, and they will sap a lot of your time and attention. A lot of us don't have ninety days to focus on only one project at the expense of everything else. That's why those of us at Evolve Global Publishing Services have another option for busy people who know they want a book, but just can't find 5 to 10 hours a week to work on it.

Evolve Global Publishing Services is a 5-step system for small business owners, entrepreneurs, authors, speakers, consultants, coaches, and professionals just like you to create your platform and become recognized as the go-to expert, authority, and star in your niche. Additionally, the program brings you the wisdom of over a dozen experts who have used these same strategies to build their brands and businesses, and succeed in a diverse array of fields.

We have a hybrid process that is designed to take you from an idea to being a published author and at least a top-10 best-seller in less than 90 days!

There is no need for you to write a single word. In most cases, it only takes around 10 to 15 hours of your time in the entire process over one to two months. We will record your words and get them transcribed to create the initial content for your book. After that, you will work one-on-one with our editor to complete the final version.

OUR UNIQUE 5-STEP SYSTEM — IN AS LITTLE AS 90 DAYS!

Our easy 5-step system is for small business owners, entrepreneurs, authors, speakers, consultants, coaches, and professionals just like you to create your platform and become recognized as the go-to expert, authority, and star in any niche.

THE 90-DAY PLAN

The system that we use to create and publish books from the ground up is discussed in detail in this book.

We'll take you from designing your book, to creating your book, to publishing and promoting your book so it becomes a #1 international best-seller. Finally, we'll teach you how to evolve your book to the next level. This system was designed with a 90-day deadline in mind, but it can be adapted for use in projects without a definitive deadline.

This book is meant to be used as a recipe guide, taking you step-by-step through the process of creating a delicious and fully-formed souffle. We'll be discussing what to avoid and things to consider along the way.

Here is a great marketing secret when it comes to promoting your book: it's common for most authors to write a book and then focus on marketing once it's done. We believe that doing it that way means you lose valuable time during those 90 days; time that if you were using, would give you massive advantages once your book is finally ready.

In Amazon, when you go to upload your book, you can choose "pre-order", which means all you need is a cover and a basic book outline to have your book active and available for sale before your launch date. You can set the release date for approximately 90 days' time. This means potential customers could be buying your book as a "pre-order", similar to pre-ordering the latest Halo game or Marvel movie. Whilst they can't read your book, allowing for "pre-orders" means you can grow your audience during the 90 days. If you list your book categories as well, you could even achieve best-seller status before your book has even been written!

We actually followed the same formula for this book, and we achieved best-seller status via pre-orders in two countries over two months before we even finished writing it. Yes, this is a surprising truth!

But this "pre-order" idea comes with a BIG WARNING: if you fail to deliver your book on time, Amazon will essentially ban you from doing it again for a year. Worse, they will tell everyone who bought your book that you missed the deadline. So, DO NOT choose this path unless you are confident you will reach your goal; or worst case, if you're worried, then wait until you've created a significant amount of the book content and only then offer it on "pre-order".

Once your "pre-order" is live, you can start promoting it and getting immediate buyers for your book. This means you can also start talking about the book with your friends and business associates. It's not an uncommon story to hear about an author who got new customers off the back of their pre-order book.

The bonus here is that Amazon re-runs the sales on your actual launch day, which helps your sales rankings to achieve #1 best-seller.

You can now spend the next 60 to 90 days building interest in your book, and this leads us to another secret in publishing: you need your own "platform". Most potential authors don't realise that a traditional publisher will ask, "What sort of platform do you have?"

Of course, you have no idea what that is! Basically, it is referring to the number of followers you have on social media, email lists, etc., and their general awareness of you as your own brand.

So as soon as you start your book journey, start working on building your own "platform" by growing a following around you, you and the topic of your book, and/or your book. One of the best ways is to create a Facebook or LinkedIn group around the book or your subject matter. Get them involved in the process, ask them to give you feedback on your cover and title ideas. Even ask them to help you at the book-launch time to buy and review your book.

THE 90-DAY PLAN IN TIMEFRAMES

Now onto the 90-day plan for creating your book—use the timeframes below as a guide for how much time you should be dedicating to each step of the process:

DAYS 1–30

The first 20 to 30 days will be devoted to designing your book. This means considering your target audience and writing your book outline. You will figure out your title, sub-title, and design your cover. Lastly, you will write your table of contents and get ready to start working on the actual content. You should also engage a good cover designer to create an eye-catching cover.

DAYS 31–80

The next 50 days should be dedicated to writing your book, using any current assets you have, as well as recording and transcribing your new content. You should then engage an editor and proofreader to help finish your book to a professional standard. Once completed, you will get the book formatted and ready for publishing.

DAYS 81–90

The final step is to publish and market your book to achieve best-seller status.

Don't worry if you get lost or confused; make sure you grab our FREE "Secret Publishing Kit" from:
www.evolveglobalpublishing.com/spk

STEP 1: DESIGNING YOUR BOOK

Before jumping into the process, brainstorm all the benefits of what a book can do for you. How will it enhance your life? What will it do for others? If you're already published, think of how you can use your book to develop products and build a business.

Some examples of what you can do with a book:

- Test a product in only 45 days.
- Develop a product roadmap.
- Obtain free traffic and leads from Amazon.
- Grow your email list from 500 to 5,000 or from 20,000 to 200,000.
- Get celebrity endorsements.
- Generate multiple streams of income.
- Land paid speaking gigs.
- Get on television.
- Become an expert resource or expert witness.

The **DESIGNING** stage will cover:

- Deciding the type of book you should write: legacy-oriented or logic-oriented
- Setting expectations for what you want your book to accomplish for you
- Basing your book around a blueprint or framework
- Defining the customer journey
- Determining how to tell your story
- Creating a good title and subtitle
- Creating an awesome cover for your book (and what to avoid)
- Learning how to write a real and effective bio

Before you can start writing your book, you need to lay the groundwork. So, if you're ready, let's get started!

Legacy or Logic

A very important question to ask yourself very early in the book creation process is, "what sort of book am I writing?" Often without realising it, people will create a "legacy" book.

Choose wisely and be very clear about what the book is designed to achieve once it is written and published.

What Is a Legacy Book?

You probably already know the answer. It's a book about yourself, but this could also extend to being a book about what you do and why you do it. The danger here is in creating a book that is based too much on ego and not enough on real content. This type of book is hard to pull off if you don't already have a following or community. Unless they care about your journey, they will never want to read your book.

One of our most successful authors, Michael Crossland wrote *Kids Don't Get Cancer*. This book is an excellent example of a legacy book. Let's look at why.

Michael had already built a successful speaking career before he wrote his book. So, after writing his book, he can sell copies of it at his presentations with the profits going to his charities. Michael has an inspiring story, and a lot of his content was created using his existing speeches. This meant the content was already "road-tested" with audiences. Michael already had a following hungry to learn more about his life and battles, and he even based his book around his key-note presentation. His story was designed to inspire and worked well as a book to expand on the subject.

More often than not, you will be starting from the virtual unknown, so unless you have a very powerful story that the book can leverage, writing this type of book can be hard to sell long-term.

We normally recommend that you **don't** write a legacy book first. It can be a huge time trap, and it's often faster and easier to write a logic book. Legacy books can become very emotional and drawn-out projects, and because of that, we feel that it's better to establish your authority first with what you are best at.

In some cases, you may plan to write a series of books. In that instance, a legacy book could be the first book in the series to help set the scene and establish your personal story.

WHAT IS A LOGIC BOOK?

A logic book is often much easier to write because it's typically based around your knowledge and experience. It's a faster book to write and has the best chance of success because you can speak to your best prospect and show them you understand their needs and wants.

Some examples of logic books include:

- How-to books
- Compilations of interviews with people on a common theme
- Thought leadership books

In the case of a logic book, try not to cover an entire subject. Rather, pick something that can be easily understood and implemented. You might want it to outline steps 1 and 2. For the final steps, readers must come to you. However, even in the process of outlining steps 1 and 2 in the book, you're selling readers on the idea that they might need some help and that you are the go-to person to help them.

Sometimes authors combine a legacy and logic book together, perhaps spending a few initial chapters on their story and then moving onto their logic blueprint. It's a great idea to do this for at least one chapter, but remember, your reader came for your insights, not necessarily inspiration.

Book Length

Writing a logic book can be a great way to test a concept or theory on a potential market. It doesn't have to be a huge book either. Even 50-page books can work to give you a starting position. Amazon has observed that the more pages a book has, the less likely it is a reader will finish the book. So, 50- to 180-page books have a much better chance than 200- to 300-page books.

You may ask, "How long does a book need to be?"

The short answer: "As long as it needs to be". While it's good to be aware of the shortcomings of different-sized books (which we cover elsewhere in this book), don't fall into the trap of padding a book out just to make it fit a certain size.

There are 10-page books on Amazon they sell very well. In fact, there is a book called *What Men Know about Women* that sells well, and it's totally blank!

THE REAL STRATEGY

What do you really want from your book?

This sounds like a simple question, but more often than not, many authors actually don't have an endgame in mind for their book. It might have started as a great idea. Their ego may have led them to write it. Then, when it's published, they realised that there was never an actual strategy around the book.

We talk about creating a book marketing plan in a later chapter, but in reality, you should draw up your marketing plan before you write a single word!

This is what that means: when writing your book, think about that one perfect prospect; your best client. Write your book as if you are talking to that one ideal client. Trying to appeal to the masses might be viable for a fiction book, but for a non-fiction book, you want engaged readers that feel the book is written just for them. It's a great idea to write down what your perfect reader looks like in terms of demographics, as well as what their personality is and what they want.

THE JOURNEY

Next, you need to know what sort of journey you want to take them on. Do you want to convince them that your ideas have value, and they should contact you for more? Of course—that's obvious!

Here is your chance to impress them with their experience with you so far. For example, do you lead them to a book bonus to continue their discovery? Or is your book the one-stop, all-in-one complete guide?

It's hard to get rich just on book royalties. For most authors, the real value of their book is in opening doors to other opportunities. Generally, a book by an entrepreneur is designed to start a conversation with the reader, engage them, and get them to sign up to talk more with you. But sometimes, that same entrepreneur doesn't have anything to sell them. Now, this could be considered a failure of "real strategy".

This is true for Michael Crossland's book, *Kids Don't Get Cancer* (one of our highest-selling books) in that he doesn't have a back-end product. His strategy is to sell his book from the back of the room. Of course, that's a great income source, but his endgame is to get more speaking engagements. His audience is likely to have prospects for other corporates who might approach him to speak at their events. Michael does have an audiobook as well, which helps increase his average sales, and it appeals to other buyers who prefer not to read.

Consider the way you will use your book, how people will discover you, and if your focus is on digital or physical copies of your book.

We have another client, Dr. Warrick Bishop, who wrote a book called *Know Your Real Risk of Heart Attack*. Originally Dr. Bishop planned to sell his books for $34.95. That's how he thought he would spread his message. But the challenge is that the cost to get a sale of the book, coupled with administration and shipping, makes it an expensive strategy to implement.

So, we took a different approach and decided to build a funnel for the ebook for $4.95. We upsell the audiobook for $9.95, and around 20 to 30% of the traffic will buy the upsell. With this strategy, we found that offering the paperback as an upsell to an eBook just didn't work. This was mainly because of digital-first readers who don't like physical books, but see an audiobook as an additional or complementary option.

The funnel then leads them to join his Healthy Heart Network Membership site. This means he has a complete customer journey from the book to an eventual recurring membership.

The system is mostly automated, and we don't have to ship a product, which means instant delivery to the purchaser.

If it costs $5 to make a sale for the book, Dr. Bishop breaks even for his marketing and everything else is a bonus. His focus is then on how to drive traffic to his automated system, which delivers the rest.

Another way is a "free + shipping" option, where you offer them the book for free, and they pay for shipping. It's a low-cost way to get a physical book into their hands. It's certainly powerful, as digital books can easily be lost or forgotten, whereas a physical book rarely gets thrown out.

However, you need to take into account the logistics and costs to make this happen, as well as the customer service to handle any lost books, etc. This is really good for volume sales or when you have an established following already.

Perhaps bookstores are your target distributor. This involves a lot of leg work: contacting the bookstore buyers, organising in-store promotions and book signings. Getting your book stocked in traditional bookstores can be a long and involved process, so you need to be prepared for that.

Lastly, you could be selling your book for full RRP (recommended retail price). If your book is valuable, there is no reason why you can't command full price for it. But to do this, you need good marketing and sales pages, or a process like Michael Crossland has by selling them at the back of the room.

So, for example, consider this: you decided to create a 300-page book and then found out after it was printed that it was a few grams overweight and cost 20% more for shipping. This would make the whole physical project unviable.

Spend some time thinking about how your book will be used, what formats you will push the most, and any potential issues that may arise along the way. On the front end, it's worth it for you to consider both the journey you want your ideal client to take in reading the book as well as the journey you'll be taking to get the book and additional services and products to them.

BLUEPRINTS AND FRAMEWORKS

Writing a book can also help you gain more clarity around your business or product/service. We have worked with many entrepreneurs who come with an idea for a book only to find that they have totally changed their mind a few weeks later. This is because once you start writing a book, your mind wants it to make sense to the reader. This can create a great opportunity to re-think your business process or framework.

On top of that, sometimes your book can be the framework for a whole new business. When we wrote, *The 5 Stages to Entrepreneurial Success*, this book explained our whole business system and concepts, so later we could make a course and mastermind around it. This method means you are creating a bigger asset for your business.

It's also important to decide how much of your IP you should put in your book. Authors are fearful that their ideas will be stolen, or they will reveal too much to a potential prospect who will go and do it themselves instead.

It's highly likely that your best prospect for your business may not even read your book extensively, and really, they just want the peace of mind that you know what you're doing.

At the same time, someone could (assuming you have given them the complete blueprint) use your book completely without you.

So, making a decision about what to leave out of the book is an important task and should be considered during the book-writing process.

One of the best ways to extend your book is to have bonus material that they need to swap for their email address. This bonus material could consist of cheat sheets, checklists, or video content.

You could then lead them to paid courses, consultations, coaching, and mastermind groups.

Make a list of what assets you have right now that could be useful bonuses that you could offer in your book.

In some cases, the actual creation of your book content could be a bonus. Some of our authors have recorded their content on audio or video as part of the book creation process. These audios or videos could be used as a "behind the scenes" bonus.

On the subject of blueprints, it's a good idea to think about these concepts in bite-sized chunks. When we wrote this book, we broke our process into 5 distinct areas or steps. So, try for 3, 5, or 7 steps. Beyond that, you are starting to get into a deeper process that might be hard for a reader to comprehend.

Once we established our 5 steps, we could then framework the book and fill in the gaps, which made writing a lot easier overall. After we fleshed out the 5 steps, all we had to do was write an introduction and an ending and we were done!

Lastly, consider how your framework might work graphically, meaning how you can represent your framework to readers in the form of an image. In *The 5 Stages to Entrepreneurial Success* we hired a graphic artist to design the stages as cartoon people.

But be warned: this can suck a lot of time out of your project. We probably spent 3 to 4 weeks just getting this right. But it was worth it because we could re-use the images for the cover and websites, etc.

We ended up with over 32 images because we had male and female characters in separate graphics, then together, and eventually as part of an overall image.

Here is an example:

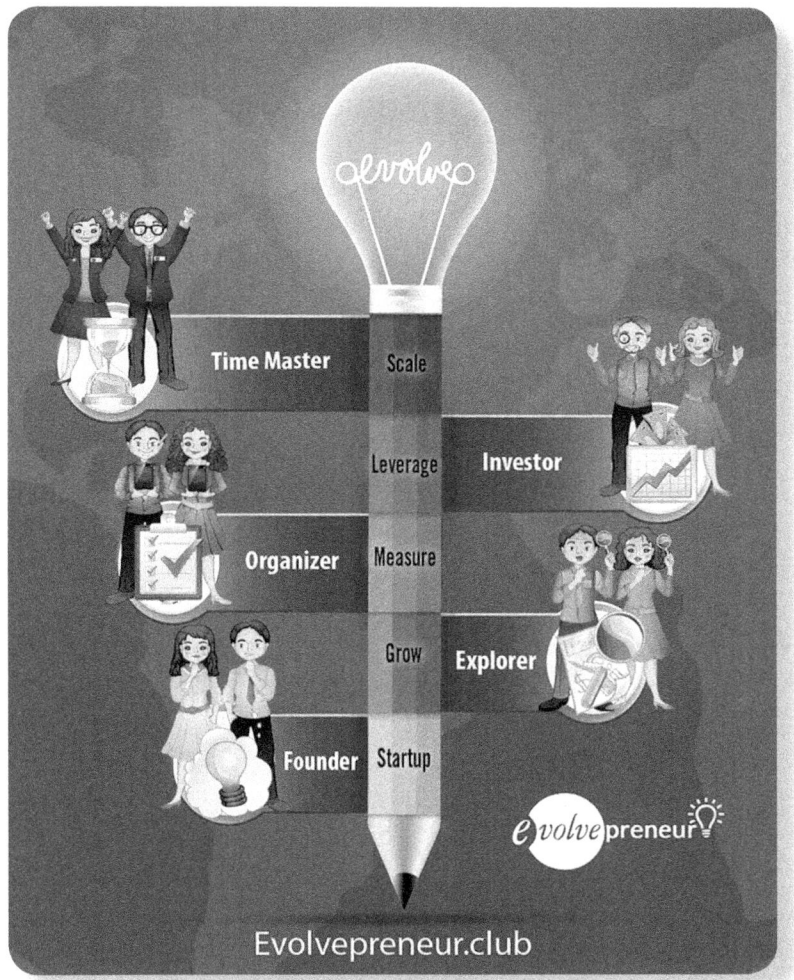

Creating your book around this concept of a blueprint or framework will not only make it easier to write, but it may also put you on a path of clarity for marketing purposes.

Take some time out to sit and think about this chapter and how you could incorporate this concept into your book.

Customer Journey

Your book is a vehicle for your customer journey.

Your future customers will go from having a need—"I need to improve my marketing"—to doing the research—"This book seems to have good information"—to consideration—"The author seems to know what they're doing. I'll look into their services".

Because you are providing information for those interested in your field of business, you are involved with them from stage one. Being both an expert and a service provider is a powerful position to be in.

Most of the time, businesses are able to control the consideration stage by setting up beautiful websites with relevant information. However, it's far less common to be able to be an important part of the research stage. Having a published book, however, marks you as an expert, which means you are a valuable source of information for potential customers in the research stage. It's often said that 70% of the customer's journey is complete before they even reach out to sales. And because of that, the customer's journey is an important framework for your marketing strategy.

The Research Stage

At this point, the customer has a need, but they don't know how to satisfy it.

Therefore, they will do research to find a service that will satisfy their need. Many go first to Google, looking for educational material and testimonials. These are the exact type of things that you need to have available for the potential customer to look at to progress to the consideration stage.

It's generally not that hard to get some testimonials from your clients and display them on your website, but creating educational material requires more work. Blogs are a good light-weight way of publishing educational content. But customers will likely be looking for something more substantial, which is what your book is for.

You should promote your book before you display your testimonials on your website. Your willingness to provide valuable information to the customer is a great way of getting off on the right foot.

As customers are finishing up the research stage, they will start to narrow down their choices based on which services best fit what they're looking for. Then they'll move into the consideration stage.

THE CONSIDERATION STAGE

After surveying all of the information available on their field of interest, they'll start looking into the few service providers that have remained on their radar. They'll investigate how each of them addresses their issues.

Potential customers will start directly and deeply comparing the products/services between each company's offerings.

Then, a question arises in them: "Why should I choose your service over someone else's?"

This answer can depend on customer service/support, time to implement the solution, your experience, or the cost of the product or service.

Most customers will naturally favour the service provider that appears more professional and has more experience. The best way to signal this is by directing potential leads to your book. It says that you are an expert, you're willing to share valuable information with those interested in it, and you have a lot of experience.

Additionally, it will appear on your customer's radar early in the research stage, so you have a leg up on competitors that don't have a published book.

Having a published book can be what gets you the sale if you position and market yourself right.

What's Your Story?

One of the major assets you need in your marketing arsenal is a great personal story. You can use this story in your "About the Author" page in your book, the back cover, and anywhere you market your book.

Your story needs to be consistent, entertaining, and easy for someone else to retell.

There are several parts to developing your personal story to help position yourself as an expert in your industry.

Ask Yourself "Why?"

Understanding why you do what you do is the key factor that will help you position yourself. At the end of the day, the "what" only matters to the few, but the real reason "why" you do what you do is a powerful narrative to your audience.

You will find, for anyone who is famous, most know their "key story". It's probably focused around overcoming adversity to be hugely successful. Even in movies, you see what is called "the hero's journey", which is where you see the hero suffer through trials and tribulations in order to eventually achieve their goal.

Personal Narrative

The first step is to develop your personal narrative.

The ultimate outcome of designing your narrative is to help your audience identify with you and understand what you stand for.

You may do exactly the same thing as thousands of other experts do, but it's your unique story that allows people to get to know you. This is how they will begin to know, like, and trust you. The idea is to create an emotional connection that instantly differentiates you from other authors in your field.

As an author, speaker, and story consultant Robert McKee explained it:

Stories are the creative conversion of life itself into a more powerful, clearer, more meaningful experience. They are the currency of human contact.

What's Your "Hook"?

A "hook" is a specific piece of your story designed to get attention. For example, one of our authors got cancer at the age of one, and was given a 1% chance of survival. Does this make you want to find out more?

We would say that most people would respond, "What?! Tell me more!"

To put you out of your misery, that hook came from the book *Kids Don't Get Cancer*, available on Evolvepreneur.club's bookstore.

What's Your Personal Story?

The goal of having a personal story is to attract your ideal target market and repel anyone who is not. Now, a lot of people struggle with the notion that you'd want to repel anyone from doing business with you. Yet, in reality, you'll have much better, faster results if you target only your ideal customers and set yourself up to work with just the exact, right people.

Decide on a message or theme, and use this as your primary blueprint for the signature story.

Talk to "the one perfect customer" and then practice delivering your story as if you're talking to that person.

BOOK TITLE AND SUBTITLE

Your book title and subtitle are vital, but are often the most undervalued step in the publishing process. Often, authors don't spend much time generating ideas for these parts of their books. Instead, they settle on the first one that comes to mind.

We will often brainstorm 100 titles before deciding on the best one. Seriously.

It is often on the strength of your title that readers decide whether or not to consider buying your book. The only other thing that comes close is your cover, which we will speak about more in the next chapter, "Designing an Awesome Cover".

What makes a good title?

Generally, most titles are 7 words or less, and ideally, they're 3 words or less. Because they take up so much of the cover, you want your title to be easy for the reader to say.

One of the best ways to get ideas for your title is to look through your own library, the bookstore, or on Amazon, and make a list of all the titles that grab you. Millions of books have already been published, so take inspiration from them.

Make sure your title is:

- **Simple, short, and clear.** First impressions are instant. When a reader sees a book with a bad title, their body instantly recoils as they're reading it. By the same token, when a reader loves a book title, their eyes dance with joy. You want readers to instantly and instinctively fall in love with your book before they want to buy it—don't make them read more than 8 words just to process your title. And don't make it overly complicated, or readers will be left simply confused. You want it to be easy to remember and easy to say. So keep it simple, keep it short, and make sure its meaning is immediately clear.

- **Specific and relevant to your book's content.** In an attempt to simplify the title, some authors end up with a vague and unclear title. It isn't clear who they're targeting and what their book is about. For a reader to believe there's value in reading your book, they need to understand what it's about. So, if your book is specifically about retraining your staff to adapt to new technologies, don't name it *Adapting to Change*. It's too vague—it sounds more like a psychology book than a business book. Don't set up false expectations for readers on what your book is about. If your target audience is small and niche, don't try to appeal to everyone. Attract your target audience, and repel everyone else.

- **Able to be used as a domain name ... and hasn't been used before.** This will come into greater relevance when we get to the **PROMOTING** stage, but you want to have your title available as a domain name so that you can create a website designed specifically to sell your book. The URL should, ideally, be [your title] + .com. So make sure it isn't taken. It is also crucially important that the title you want to use for your book has not already been used for another book. Your title needs to be unique.

You should not spend all your time on coming up with one good book title, however. The very first thing you should do is make a list of all the keywords relevant to your topic(s), and come up with 20 to 30 titles that use those keywords. Immediately get rid of all the ones that just don't click, and keep the ones that have potential. Work on improving the better ones and removing the ones that don't work.

Don't worry about spending too much time on your title unless you've been at it for a month and still haven't been able to settle on a title. At some point, you're going to have to pick something. This is one of the most important parts of creating your book, so don't brush it off as something you can "think about later". It will appear in every single promotion for your book, it will reflect your business's brand, you will probably use it on your bio, and it will be difficult to change later. You do not want to be stuck with a bad book title.

So, spend some time on it, and ask for feedback from others too.

Your subtitle, however, is a drastically different case from your title. Generally, three words is the minimum, and it serves as a short description of your book. Keywords are particularly important for page ranking on Google and other search engines. While it should be descriptive, you should also be trying to put as many relevant keywords into the subtitle as possible to attract people searching for topics you cover in your book.

Your subtitle should be long and descriptive, but it should also be specific and relevant, just like your title. You should make a promise of a benefit that the reader will receive if they read your book. For *Book Publishing Secrets for Entrepreneurs*, this was "Create an International Best-Selling Book." It piques the reader's interest, and it gets them excited about reading the book.

The subtitle has the job of explaining what the book is really about, and the title is focused on grabbing the reader. You should include your framework or success blueprint in your title/subtitle, if you have one. For example, "Without Writing a Single Word". It gives the reader an idea of what you're going to write about without giving them any answers.

The subtitle is less important than the title, but you should spend a similar amount of time on it and try out a number of different subtitles to see what works best.

Designing an Awesome Cover

Now it's time to work on your book cover. This can be a daunting and time-consuming task, but if you break it down into pieces and take your time, your cover will be amazing. Rushing your book cover is not recommended.

The cover is arguably the most important part of your book because it is the very first impression of your book that a prospective reader will get. And if you're not careful, it will be the only impression of your book they get.

When you walk into a bookstore, but you don't quite know what you're looking for, you will search the entire store (or at least your favourite categories) for something that you think will be worth your time and money. If your eyes land on an amateur or unappealing cover, you're likely to dismiss it immediately, and you haven't even read the first word!

When you talk about your book, when your readers think about your book, when they see your book, when you give a client your book, when you promote your book, and when people think about you, the image in their minds will be your book cover. It's important to get it right.

Your book cover is not a nice extra: it is *the* primary representation of your book, and it will largely be what convinces somebody to pick up (or put down) your book. You do not want to give a bad first impression of your book by making one of these very common mistakes:

#1 The title should be the most prominent part of your cover. For many people, the first place they see your book will not be in a physical bookstore; it will likely be online. What this means is that they will first see your book as a small thumbnail. If your title is too small, they won't know what your book is about, and they won't be interested in it. There are very few cases where a title is too big for a book. More often than not, it could stand to be bigger. It should be the first thing you see on the cover.

#2 Use a maximum of three fonts on the front cover. This will usually be one font for your main title, one font for your subtitle, and the last font for any miscellaneous text (i.e., review excerpts, awards, best-seller badges, etc.). The name of the author should usually use the same font as the main title. For some reason, it's very common among self-published authors to use 3 or 4 different fonts in the same small space. This is a bad practice for a few reasons. The first is that it makes your cover incoherent. When a reader sees a cover with 5 different fonts, some bolded, some italicized, all different colours, their first instinct is to look away. They don't know where to look because there are no cues as to which text is most important. Good designs lead the eye around the cover, from the most important information to least important.

Some good guidelines are:

- The title should be the biggest and blockiest font on the cover because it's the most important and the reader shouldn't miss it.
- The subtitle should be less than half the size of the title and is generally the least important text on the cover. The font shouldn't be as blocky as the title so that it's easier to read.
- The name of the author should use the same blocky text as the title but not be as big. This is the second

most important information on the cover, but it usually always goes on the bottom because that is where the reader naturally looks for the name of the author.

- Any other text, such as awards or review text, should usually be in a serif font like Times New Roman.

#3 Use professional fonts. Please don't use Calibri for your title and Arial for your subtitle. Helvetica is also a poor choice. Times New Roman is okay for award/ miscellaneous text, but if you have something better, use it. The reason you shouldn't use these fonts, or many of the fonts pre-installed on your computer, is because it makes your book look common and unprofessional. Anyone who browses the internet often has seen those fonts a million times over. They don't want to see them anymore. They're also not very good fonts to put on your front cover because that's not what they were designed for. Instead, use professional fonts, the fonts that graphic designers rely on. You can find them, on font sites or you can use Adobe's large library of fonts. If you don't know what they are, there are plenty of sites happy to tell you which fonts are the best for which job. Sometimes you have to pay for a good-looking font, but it's often worth the price to leave a good first impression on a prospective reader.

#4 Make sure your text is readable. The more complicated your cover, the bigger an issue this is. If you are placing text over a background with varying colours, make sure you can actually read the text without having to squint. Don't use incompatible colours like bright yellow text on a red background, blue text on a purple background, or dark red text on a black background. Be especially careful with the use of yellow text because it often strains the eyes to look at.

#5 Be smart about colour. You don't have to be an expert at spinning the colour wheel, but it's a good idea to plan your use of colour sparingly. Make sure you have a primary and secondary colour that are compatible with each other. Try to have a tertiary colour as well. The primary colour is usually the general colour of your (primary) background, and the secondary colour is typically the colour of your most important text and can be a secondary background colour. The tertiary colour can be used for less important text and for emphasising certain aspects of the cover. You don't really need any more or less colours than this though a subtle fourth colour can help create some definition when used intelligently. Two colours is the absolute minimum and is suitable for a simpler cover.

When you use colour in this way, you are not only creating good contrast, but you are also telling the brain what information is the most important based on the size and colour of elements. This is great for establishing coherence in your cover design.

#6 Stay simple. This is something a lot of self-published books fail to get. The impression is that the more complex the cover is, the more professional it looks, when the opposite is true. The more moving parts there are, the trickier it is to get them all working in synchronicity. This is true in anything; not just cover design. Just look at some of Stephen King's covers for great examples of both fantastic and awful cover design. You'll notice that the simplest covers—the new *It* cover, *The Outsider* cover, and the new *Firestarter* cover—are much more appealing than the over-designed ones—the old *Firestarter* cover, the *Night Shift* cover, and the *Under the Dome* cover.

The over-designed ones are almost like magazine covers, with huge text strewn across the cover, and the background is typically very complicated. It's hard to know where to look and what to read because it overwhelms prospective readers. Stephen King's simplest covers follow a similar formula: the cover is predominately in one colour (for *It*, white; for *Firestarter* red); there is a small, simple image in the center of the cover that represents the primary fear the novel exploits; and his name is in huge text at the top, followed by the title of the book at the bottom. And, if it warrants it, the best-seller text goes at the very top, and the review excerpt goes at the very bottom.

The philosophy behind this design is to think about what your cover needs at the very minimum, and then create that. If you need to incorporate more elements, think carefully about which ones you really need because each extra element will decrease the overall coherence of your cover.

#7 Use images that you actually own. DO NOT use images that you have found using Google images unless you know that you can use it based on the copyright license. Because other parties own these images, you are typically not free to use them without permission in your own work. Using images that you don't own without permission to use or modify it is a very easy way to get sued. This applies to images both on the cover and inside the book, and in any other creative project, usually. Getting permission to use images can be very difficult, and copyright holders may ask you to take down the image later anyway, so this is not a very good way of getting images for your cover.

Instead, if you want to use images that you didn't create, you can create an account on a stock photo website like Shutterstock and purchase the images there for use in your book. This way, you own the images and you can modify them as you like (unless specified otherwise). Alternatively, you can hire someone to do the images you want for your book though this is naturally more expensive.

#8 Use high-quality images, not clip art. If you do want to use images on your cover, don't use clip art that you can find on programs like Word or on some royalty-free clip art site, because it's not very good. You get what you pay for, right? Source your images from a professional stock photo site or hire somebody to do your images for your book specifically if you are really concerned about quality. The impression you are trying to create for your readers is that this book is worth their time. It is very difficult to accomplish this with cheap clip art, so we highly recommend you either create the images in-house or use images from Shutterstock or similar sites.

#9 Don't put your name at the top of your book. A reader will always look for your name at the bottom of the book, because that is where it has been, historically, for as long as they can remember. A rare breed of authors will put their name at the top of their book, but this is only for widely recognised authors where their name means more than anything else. Stephen King, for example, has a habit of putting his name at the top of his books because he is so prominent. Because he dips into so many experimental areas as an author, a reader who sees the title and cover may not be interested in it, but if they see "Stephen King" printed in bold letters at the top, they might well pick it up. Most people are not Stephen King, so seeing an author's name at the top of their book does nothing for readers.

#10 Brand your book properly. Your book is a representation of you, especially if you are on the front or back cover. Your book influences your branding whether you want it to or not, so it's important that you get it right. Make sure that the photo you use is good. We mean this in several ways. Your photo should be of high quality, but it should also be a good representation of you. If you don't usually sport a beard, don't use a photo where you have a beard. Don't use an old photo. If you are writing a book for your business, make sure that most of the colours on your cover are the same as your logo, or very similar.

#11 Make sure your cover has the right specifications for print. Don't start designing your cover until you have the specifications at hand. You need to know the resolution and the cut-off areas for the spine and front and back covers, so that you don't put important elements over them or underestimate the size of the spine. You also need to make sure you can produce the right file type using your program(s), which will probably be Illustrator, Photoshop, and InDesign. You don't want to end up with your cover done but unable to submit it because your specifications are wrong. You may even need to start over at that point.

#12 Get feedback! When you're done with your cover, you need to know if your target market will actually like it. So, you need to get feedback on the design. A great way to do this is to find a group, possibly on Facebook, to show your cover to. Getting outside opinions is crucial for creating an awesome cover design—because you may think it looks good, but your readers may not agree with you.

#13 Don't design your own book cover. You are probably not the best person to design your own cover, in much the same way you are probably not the best person to do your own editing. Even for graphic designers, unless you are showcasing your work, you probably shouldn't be doing your own covers. The reason is very simple: you are too close to your own work to see the flaws. Following a checklist or guide like this can make creating a good design yourself more realistic, but truly good design is something you can *just feel*; bad design is trickier to identify. Sometimes it's just the absence of that feeling you get when you see a good cover, and other times it's something that sticks out, or something that doesn't. When you're so close to the work, it's easy to downplay those things, but months afterward, it will be at the forefront of your mind whenever you look at your cover.

So, the more distance you can get from your cover, the better you will be for it. It's a good idea to have a list of things you want to include on your front cover to be able to hand to a designer, and then have them interpret your specifications in a way you would never have thought of. And because of your distance from the cover, you'll be able to see and offer solutions for fixing those little things that have a big impact.

#14 Know when to break the rules. Keep in mind that these are only guidelines for how you should design your cover, and therefore not absolutes. These are rules that we stick to as closely as possible, but sometimes we have to break them to improve the cover depending on the circumstances. It is ultimately up to you to decide what works and what doesn't because good design is not necessarily based on a formula. Sometimes the best covers are the ones that break the rules well. So long as you have a good enough reason to do something that outweighs the risk, it's alright to break the rules.

GETTING YOUR COVER DONE

Even if you aren't planning on designing your own cover, it's important to keep these things in mind for when you are reviewing a design someone else has done for you. Designing an awesome cover is the most important thing you can do for your book. You should start doing this as soon as you know your target market: know what you want to say and have your title. But this doesn't mean that you have to complete this before you start working on the content of your book.

In actuality, if your cover is being done by a designer (which we recommend you do), you will be spending most of your time creating the content of your book and periodically reviewing the cover design to make sure that everything is coming along properly. So long as the content of and ideas behind your book don't change (which, if you've planned it properly, they won't), these are two entirely separate processes after you have finalised your strategy.

To help out your designer, it's a good idea to write out a list of what you want and don't want on your cover; these are your **design specifications**. These are things such as:

- A short description of your book
- Your full name as you want it on the cover
- Your target market
- The size of your physical book (we usually recommend 6x9)

- Whether you want your face on the cover
- Whether you want light or dark colours
- Three colours you want to explore
- The style you're looking for; e.g., business, serious, retro, sleek, simple, cartoony, etc.
- Any images you want on the cover
- Anything specific to avoid
- Some back cover text: endorsements, bio, etc.
- Whether you want your author picture on the back

Design Schedule

While you shouldn't rush your cover design, it's also important that you don't spend months on it. If you are constantly second-guessing yourself, you will never get it done. That's why we try to aim, with every book we do, to complete the cover design in 14 days. You should also be able to follow this schedule with your own designer:

Day 1

This is the day where you will do the bulk of the work for the cover. The first thing you need to do is create a list of things that you need on the cover. These are the design specifications we talked about earlier. Try to spend some time researching other covers in your field/genre to see if there are aspects you want to take and try out for your own cover. Once you're done, ask your designer to create 3 or more designs that match these specifications.

Days 2 and 3

Your designer will work on the specifications they are given to design three or more distinct covers.

DAY 4

Out of the 3 or more designs that your designer has done for you, pick 2 covers that you really like and want to continue with (and only 3 if you really think they're all great). Naturally, your designer probably hasn't done everything exactly the way you want them to do it, so you will need to hand them over some major changes for them to incorporate into the cover. This is what they will spend the next two days doing.

DAYS 5 AND 6

Your designer will take your feedback and work on improving the selected covers.

DAY 7

When you receive the covers back with the changes made, go over them again for any changes you may have missed in the first round. These changes will probably be of a more minor nature. Ask for these changes to be done and ask for your designer to create the rest of the cover (spine and back cover) now with placeholder text on the back cover.

DAYS 8 AND 9

Your designer will fix up any issues and work on creating the entire cover (back cover and spine).

DAY 10

The spine and back cover are less tricky than the front cover, so they probably won't need that much work. You need to supply the designer with the text you want on the back cover and any changes you want to make to it. You also need to make sure that the spine is okay and matches the text on the front cover. It should only include the title (not the subtitle) and your name.

Days 11 and 12

Your designer will finalise the cover and give you back the final files, including an image of the front cover.

Day 13

Now that you've reached the final stage of designing your cover, you should be happy with the remaining cover variations. You may have been so happy with one of the designs that you only have one remaining design left. But now it's time to put it to the test. This works better with 2 to 3 covers, but you will also get some good feedback by posting your cover to a group/forum willing to tell you what they honestly think. Ask people to vote on which cover they like the best; or if you only have one cover, ask them what they like and don't like about it.

Day 14

Based on the feedback you received the previous day, decide on which cover you want to use. If you received some heavy criticism for a certain design, take it back to the designer to change it based on that feedback. You should now have a final cover and the files you need to get it published in eBook and paperback format.

Most of the time, however, things do not go this smoothly. The designer may take longer to make certain changes; or you may realise that you missed things upon closer inspection; or you may even need to change the title halfway through. That's okay. Things happen. This 14-day schedule is only meant to be used as a guideline to give you an idea of how you should go about working on your cover. It's a back-and-forth process of creation and review: the designer works on your cover, next you review it, and then they work on it some more. The process repeats itself until it's done. Some covers may not need this many rounds of changes, while others may need twice as many.

It's important to remember that you will likely have the opportunity to re-do your cover in the future, after your book is published (so long as you don't print 5,000 books in the face of only 100 sales a month; if you do that, you'll have to get rid of those books before you print more). If you're ever planning on re-writing your book to include updated information, this is one of those opportunities. Or you may just want to update the cover after the first print run is done, adding in some minor improvements.

If you are spending a lot of time on your cover and your launch date is quickly approaching, perhaps a month away: at this point, your job is to get your cover to a stage where it is "good enough" and you can be happy with finalising it as the first-edition cover. If you've spent two months working on your cover, you need to get it to that level and focus on other aspects of your book.

The cover of your book is the most important part of your book, and it's precisely because it is that you can't spend forever designing it. You can't release a book without a cover. The truth is, in creative endeavors, there is no point when work is "done". You just reach a stopping point.

WRITING A REAL BIO

"What is the difference between a 'BIO' and a 'Real BIO'?" you may ask.

Most BIOs or biographies you will see are not that interesting and mostly talk about the person, and they're likely to endlessly list their qualifications.

In this chapter, we are discussing how to write a BIO not just for your book itself but also for general marketing purposes.

In reality, your BIO isn't really about you. It's about what you do for others. Your bio is a simple, concise, story-based summary of who you are, what you do, and your qualifications based on your experience and background. As an expert, you have a solution to a problem. When you have expertise, knowledge, or tools that people need, it is your moral and ethical obligation to deliver it.

That's the reason you are striving to position yourself as an author and expert in your industry, and share your content with your personal community, and even the wider world. The financial upside of creating your platform is a wonderful benefit, but not a driving factor.

Please don't ever doubt the value of your contributions, and move forward with confidence and the certainty of your abilities.

WHY YOU SHOULD HAVE A GOOD BIO

A powerful BIO is a key factor for your book. It will help to establish your identity in the marketplace, so you need to spend a decent amount of time on its creation.

What's Wrong with a 2,500-Word Bio?

Don't get us started on a huge BIO that sounds more like a resume than a story! Whilst we recommend you have a long BIO as part of your personal marketing assets, you need to be able to tell your story without putting the reader to sleep in the process. Don't be boring. You only get one chance to make a first impression—don't blow it.

Start with Your Unique Selling Proposition

Your Unique Selling Proposition is what differentiates you from everybody else in your field of focus. The best way to identify your unique selling proposition is to use the following formula:

"I teach X to Y even if Z."

An example of ours is this: "We help people like you to become #1 best-selling authors in less than 90 days without writing a single word."

Your Own "BIO"-Builder

We actually have a full online BIO-builder at www.evolvepreneur. club. Feel free to check that out if you are struggling to undertake this vital task.

When writing your BIO, make sure you consider these factors:

- It's not a resume.
- Be very clear about why you are different.
- Focus on your achievements in the real world.
- Be short, concise, and get rid of unnecessary words.
- Be 100% accurate.

- Avoid jargon, keep the words simple and easy to understand.
- Include social proof, especially if you have well-known people as clients.
- Mix up the sentences; don't start everyone with "Joe is ..."
- Use the third person, never the first person.

You should aim to create several versions of your BIO. You should have a really short one, say, 50 words. Then a longer one at around 250 words. Consider an even longer one that you might include in your book (in the "About the Author" chapter) and other key locations. The best way to get several versions is to first write a long one and then trim it radically to get the size down for the shorter ones.

As you cut away everything unnecessary, piece by piece, you'll end up with a few sweet and short bios that contain only the bare essentials.

Lastly, consider creating a verbal elevator pitch version of your bio that you can easily deliver when doing interviews or introducing yourself in public when you are asked: "So, what do you do?"

Make sure you practice it until it's automatic and authentic.

STEP 2:
CREATING
YOUR BOOK

It's time to start your journey to actually creating your book. We will cover all the necessary steps to getting your book content done.

The topics we cover include:

- Setting expectations
- Determining the number of pages your book should be
- Figuring out how many images you should have
- Deciding whether to print in colour or black and white
- Including a glossary
- Pinning down what to write about
- Creating chapter outlines and planning
- Creating content rapidly
- Figuring out the actual content
- Drafting and editing

There is a lot to do, but we have smart ways and our own secrets to get it done quickly. So let's get started right now.

Big Plans

Now that you've read the **DESIGNING** section, you can properly define what your book is and what you want to achieve with it. That step, more than any other, is the most important part of your book. Without the proper foundation, you will not be able to produce a professional-grade book. But if you've properly read the first section, you're already well on your way.

Before you start writing, you need to set some expectations.

Many authors jump into writing their books with big plans without fully thinking them through. This applies especially to creative writing, but no author is immune to it. These "big plans" include ideas like:

- setting a target of 400 pages
- wanting to include an exhaustive history of your business to enhance your credibility
- including detailed diagrams on every second page to ensure the reader knows what you're talking about
- bringing a long list of other experts in to re-affirm your credibility and authority

These are not necessarily bad ideas. In fact, some are great ideas—if executed in moderation. It's important to realise that a sales book is something very different to an autobiography. But an overeager author can quickly blur the lines between the two without properly thinking about their book's identity. That's why, from the outset, our **DESIGNING** section focuses on getting you to define the parameters, thrust, and themes of your book in detail.

The takeaway is that having big plans is not a bad thing— in fact, a healthy stream of ideas is the best thing for your book—but that you need to think about where it fits in for your book. Wanting to mention your business's history in a financial strategy book is a good idea, but only take the most interesting parts from it (as opposed to the complete history), and let your readers fill in the blanks. By the same token, wanting to incorporate case studies and/or testimonials to bolster your authority is an excellent idea, but don't overdo it or your readers will feel like they're being sold to. Case studies and testimonials are not the same thing, but they can achieve the same effect when used correctly.

Case Studies

Case studies are sections where you take an example from your own personal or professional experience (typically, a client you've worked with), and use the scenario to make a point and/or explain something to the reader. It's common to subtly present a client as a person with a problem and the business (your business) as the party with the solution. If you do it right, readers will come away feeling like they learned something, and some of them may think: "I know how to fix my problem, but I don't have the time. [This author's business] solves problems like that, so I'll go to them".

Creating a good sales book is about balancing marketing and educational value, which is why case studies are one of your most valuable tools in creating your book.

Testimonials

Testimonials, on the other hand, are when a client praises the business for helping them out with a problem. In their purest form, they are recommendations and implicit guarantees of quality from the client to the business. In this form, they have no educational value.

THE "SECRET" ART ...

However, the art of the sales book is all about creating testimonials from case studies. A case study can also be a testimonial, as mentioned earlier. You just have to make sure that the reader learns something from the scenario.

But for many authors, their biggest challenge isn't finding content to make up the length of the book. It's being able to choose the best content and save the rest for another project.

A balanced and engaging book is the result of a great many compromises between a myriad of big ideas. It can be easy to become attached to certain ideas, particular paragraphs, or a satisfying turn of phrase. But to write a good book, you have to be able to separate yourself from the work. If something doesn't quite fit in, and you can't find a place to include it, you need to do some cutting.

Take all of your big ideas, and examine them all one-by-one to see where they fit in for the concept for your book. If you can't fit them in, even in moderation, it's not a good idea. **Save it for the next book.**

LITTLE DETAILS

There are a myriad of details, questions, and guidelines that will affect what you write, how you write it, and the length of what you write. Ultimately, you shouldn't let the little details get in the way of writing what you want to write, but it's worth it to keep them in mind for later on in the process when you're about to publish your book.

TARGET WORDS/PAGES

For a large majority of our authors, we usually set the target word count to be around 35,000 to 40,000 words. This usually comes out to roughly 150 pages, which is long enough to be considered an extensive and valuable read, but without morphing into a textbook. It's also short enough that busy people can consider scheduling time to read it. 150 pages, or about 40,000 words, is something you can aim for if you're not sure how short or long to make your book.

There are also some other important factors that can affect the size of your book:

- A book must be at least 108 pages to have text on its spine (if your book lacks a spine, it can look amateurish and can undermine your credibility).
- The more pages a book has, the higher the cost of printing per book. And the higher the printing costs, the less of a margin you make per book. In other words, the less money you're going to make overall.

How Many Images Are Best? Should There Be Any Images At All?

Your book may have 80 images, diagrams, etc., or it may have one. You may choose to have an image to accompany the start of every new chapter. Or you may need to include several diagrams if what you're talking about is hard to explain just using words. Of course, if you're talking about something greatly complex, it may be better to just simplify the concept for the reader and only give them the footnotes. Oftentimes, it's enough for a reader to understand why something is important and the kind of process you undertake to do it. If they want more information ... they can contact you.

But back to the topic of images: you should include at least one image in your book: the author headshot. If the reader doesn't know that you're a real person, why should they care about you? Creating a book about yourself in order to boost your credibility or get your foot in the door won't work if readers don't know who you are.

It's also a good idea to include a number of other images interspersed throughout your chapters to break up the monotony of walls upon walls of text—though, depending on the type of book you're writing, this may be precisely what you want. Be careful not to take the inclusion of images too far. You're writing a book, not arranging an image gallery. If your 150-page book has 15 images, that's plenty. A good rule of thumb is to take 10% of the number of pages in your book, and limit the maximum amount of flavour images you add to that number. For example, 10% of 150 is 15 images.

If you find that you have many more images than 10% of your page count, and they add value by explaining or illustrating a concept you're writing about, that's perfectly okay. Diagrams and context images are much more important than flavour images. If you already have plenty of the former two types, it may not be strictly necessary to include flavour images at all.

Of course, if you're writing a fiction book, for example, images aren't typically a great idea. The vast majority of fiction books do not include images beyond the cover and author images because you want your reader to immerse themselves in it as much as possible. The best way to do that is to let them imagine your world in their own mind's eye. By including images that represent your imagined world, you break the reader's immersion because they see something that doesn't match up with what they imagined.

So generally, leave the images to non-fiction books.

But beyond presentation, the number of images in your book also greatly impacts your printing costs. The more images you have, the higher your cost of printing per book will go. Don't be scared away by economics if you really think your book needs something in it, but always keep it in mind when creating your book, so you don't have to cut it later.

Colour vs. Black and White

Should your images be in colour?

Would a diagram be impossible to understand without colour?

These are important questions to ask. Printing your book in colour will greatly increase the cost of printing, more than anything else.

Obviously, colour will generally improve the look of your book, but it is a big trade-off in terms of cost. This is more of a conundrum for after you've finished creating your book, but knowing about it now means you may not have to re-edit your images later.

Index

An index is a list of words or phrases ("headings") used in your book. Its associated page numbers allow readers to easily find a particular topic based on their memory of a certain word being used. It's a really useful bonus for books that may cover a lot of technical terms.

Glossary/Appendix?

At Evolve Global Publishing, a lot of our authors tend to be experts in many different specialised fields, which is a great boon for the content of the book. However, it can also get complicated when a developer starts talking about "recursion", "refactoring code", or why classes are great because of "polymorphism". This is when a glossary or an appendix comes in handy for explaining these terms. Depending on who you're writing the book for, it may very well be expected that the reader knows what these terms mean.

But often, our authors are teaching readers new things, which tends to involve new concepts, terms, and phrases. That's when an appendix may be necessary. You may instead choose to avoid using jargon altogether. It's entirely up to you.

These little details aren't things that new authors generally think about. This is mainly because they simply don't know that much about books and publishing. They know they want to write a book, and they know they want people to read their book. They assume they'll pick up these things as they stumble along the untravelled road, and they will. Only when they do learn these things, they'll have to re-write, re-design, and re-work their book accordingly. They're completely blindsided by things that didn't even cross their mind—because they're in the book writing industry, not the book publishing industry.

Knowing about these little details puts you ahead of many, many authors already in terms of getting your book published. For you, they won't come out of left field. You'll be prepared to work around them.

WHY SHOULDN'T YOU USE WORD?

The absolute biggest mistake that almost every new author makes is writing their book entirely in Microsoft Word. A Word document has to be completely stripped of all special formatting in order to be useable for an interior (i.e. the file that contains all of the text, images, etc. for the inside of your book). It's easy to come up with beautiful, complicated layouts using Word, but they cannot actually be directly used in your eBook or print book.

Word is notorious for causing weird formatting issues, so the layout and any special formatting needs to be entirely redone in a professional publishing program. Laying out a book for print is a tedious and involved process that usually takes a few days to complete properly. Having to recreate the layout and formatting results in a lot of wasted effort, as well as an extra cost.

So, what can you do?

If you use Word or Google Docs to write your book, keep the formatting simple so it's easier later to extract for layout.

Once your manuscript is complete, you will want to layout for both print and digital books, also called eBooks.

If we're talking about eBooks, there are a lot of cloud and desktop programs in the marketplace, that will help you to produce useable and well-formatted files for eBook publishing. Amazon even has special tools you can use for this task.

You could also use an outsourcer platform such as Fiverr to have someone produce both eBook and print layouts. Just make sure that you get all the original files once the project is complete so you can change them later.

We at Evolve Global Publishing have our own proprietary software, EvolveBookPublisher.com, that will help you lay out your book and write it from scratch, ready for publishing as soon as you hit "export as EPub". The great thing about software explicitly built for eBook publishing is that you know what you can and can't do. The layout you create is the layout your eBook will use. Everything you are permitted to do is available to you and anything you aren't able to do isn't.

One great benefit of EvolveBookPublisher.com is that it's designed for collaboration.

Writers, editors, authors, designers, friends—whoever you want to see and edit your book—can do so easily. Transferring files between people take time and carry the risk of becoming corrupted when transferred or opened with different software on a new computer. It also means that two people can't work on the same book at the same time.

EvolveBookPublisher.com is an online cloud solution available in your browser that requires no extra work to share your book with anyone you're working with. It also shows you how many words are in each chapter as well as how many words are in your entire book at that moment (as well as the character count).

Most programs designed for eBook publishing are not cloud-based solutions, which means you will be transferring files between multiple parties, which slows down works and risks file corruption.

THESE ARE SOME OTHER UNIQUE BENEFITS THAT EVOLVEBOOKPUBLISHER.COM PROVIDES:

1. **Identify content changes easily because any new content you write or paste into the chapter will be highlighted in green, and any content your remove will be highlighted in red.** If you want to accept these changes, you can accept them one at a time, or you can accept them all at once. This is great, because if you accidentally delete something, it highlights it in red to make it clear, instead of outright deleting it as it would in a Word document.

2. **Organise your chapters quickly and automatically generate a table of contents.** In EvolveBookPublisher, you can create new sections and place your chapters under them. If you've placed a chapter in the wrong place, you can easily move the entire chapter to another part of your book. There's no need to create a table of contents, either, as it is automatically generated and updated inside of EvolveBookPublisher whenever you export the files.

3. **Create and update the status of each chapter.** This is a particularly handy feature that you can use to inform your editor(s), "This chapter is ready for the first draft", or "This chapter is ready for the final draft". You can create your own status flags ("needs content", "to be proofed", "ready for final draft", "completed", etc.) to indicate what state your chapter is in and what information people working on your book need to know.

4. **Add comments to a particular section in a chapter.** Highlight words and then add a comment to them. You can ask your editor to redo a sentence for better clarity, or the editor can ask you what a sentence is supposed to

mean. The comments won't appear in the final exported file, and they're easy to add, easy to respond to, and easy to remove. Additionally, you can use the 'Shared Notes' tab to add notes to the entire book; they're accessible from any area of the book, not just inside of a chapter.

5. **View versioning/change history for your chapters.** Every round of changes you or your collaborators approve to a chapter can be viewed by clicking on the "Chapter History" button. From the very first version to the very last, all the versions are viewable at the click of a button.

6. **View the update history for your entire book.** By going to the "Book History" tab you can see exactly who has made what changes to your book from the very beginning to the current moment. Whether they edited a chapter or re-ordered a chapter, the date and time the change was made and the person who made the change is shown. This is very helpful to see what progress is being made on the book, as it sometimes isn't immediately obvious.

7. **Communicate with current online collaborators using the "Chat" feature.** In EvolveBookPublisher you can communicate with all collaborators of the book using the "Chat" tab. This is useful for talking to everybody at once, and you can do it right from the page you're working on.

If you'd like to know more about EvolveBookPublisher, visit EvolveBookPublisher.com.

WHAT ABOUT THE PRINT LAYOUT?

One important thing to note is that you can't do much to help with the print layout process. This usually needs to be done from scratch in a professional program like InDesign. Due to the number of weird formatting errors, any word processor can generate, when a layout is imported, it is normally easier and more efficient to create the layout from scratch.

With that said, it's easier to write your book in an eBook publishing program because it's generally very easy to lay out the print version from it. It will still take some time, however.

Word is nice, and it's a good option for short documents like blog posts or internal company files, but it is most certainly not a versatile publishing solution. So, if you're writing a book to be published, don't use Word.

What to Write About

What should you write about? It's one thing to know that you want to write a book about your business, but what exactly should you say?

What's worth reading?

What engages readers?

What type of content will connect with readers?

These types of questions are very common for entrepreneurs who are just starting out on the journey to write a book. You may have a great grasp on where to start, and where you want to end the book, but you have no idea how to get from one point to the other. Or maybe you do have some ideas, but you feel like they aren't engaging enough to write about or that they won't connect with your readers.

One of the fastest and easiest ways to create topics to talk about is by asking yourself questions about your profession. What questions are you commonly asked by customers? For a marketer, these might be questions about using Facebook to create a following, or how to get the most out of your CRM.

In many ways, non-fiction books are all about asking and answering questions that a reader might have about the topic of interest. So, the best way to get ideas for chapters and topics is by answering the common questions that your customers ask you every day. Of course you will also need to explain the answers in more detail so that the reader can understand the thought process behind it.

If you want to inject your own stories into the book, go right ahead!

Combining compelling, relatable stories with explanatory content is a great way of keeping your readers interested. Sometimes they want to hear about how something works, but other times, they want to hear about how something worked for you. You can talk about how implementing a new strategy generated twice as many new leads, or how affiliate marketing simultaneously bolstered your reputation and increased your revenue.

Success stories get readers excited about new concepts and strategies, and the opposite is just as true. If you talk about failure, like ignoring social media marketing when it first became popular and suffering for it, your readers will feel anxious about ignoring new marketing trends and strategies. However, you should form the habit of generally telling far more success stories than stories related to mishaps or failures.

When you explain how something works, you should also take care to explain why it's beneficial or important to know. "How will this affect me?" People simply won't care if it has nothing to do with them, so you need to be clear about its benefits.

Sometimes, you have to hurt your readers to get them invested. You need to tell them everything they're doing wrong before you can tell them how to fix it, so that they'll understand how the information you are providing applies to their circumstances.

The fact is, so many people are attached to doing the same things that they've always done simply because they're familiar. You can't get them invested in new ideas or ways of doing things unless you flat out tell them that they're shooting themselves in the foot.

They just won't believe you.

People respond far more dramatically to negative stimuli, so use that.

Chapter Outlines

You shouldn't start writing anything just yet.

If you haven't already got a list of chapter names, you should do that now. You can name the chapters using the same names you came up with for the topic list you made for the book. Once you've done that, you are going to do the last of the preliminary work before you begin creating the body of the book. This preliminary work is what will make it easier for you to create the content for your book.

There are authors who write off the cuff—without much planning beyond where they're going to begin the book and where they're going to end it. We highly recommend you do not do that. Planning your book does take a little extra time and means you don't immediately start writing, but planning the path of your book on the frontend can save you from a lot of headaches in the future.

Go to the first main chapter of your book, and write a 1- to a 2-sentence summary of what you plan for the chapter to be about. You could, for example, frame your chapter summary sentences like this:

"The first sentence explains the primary objective you want the chapter to achieve; for example, explaining what chapter outlines are and why they're important. The second sentence explains any secondary objectives you might have; for example, explaining how to make good chapter outlines and how to spot bad ones".

Repeat this for every single chapter in your book.

It is very common to come back to something weeks later, not remembering what exactly it is you were trying to say. This is what we're trying to prevent by recommending you create these 1- to 2-sentence chapter summaries on the front end. By doing them before you begin writing, you are placing a future reminder for yourself when you get to the point where you need to create the content for that chapter a week or two or three down the line. See it as a helpful way for you to remember what exactly it was that you wanted to say.

At the same time, you are also conceptualising each chapter into two short sentences. If you find that you're writing 100 words just to explain your chapter briefly, then it sounds like your chapter is too complex. It suggests you should consider splitting that chapter up into two chapters.

Each chapter should explore one big idea in detail, including, for example, benefits and drawbacks, how to achieve X, things to look out for, or methods for improving Z. If you're exploring two big ideas, you might be overwhelming the reader. It's always a good idea to streamline and simplify.

You can take your chapter outlines further and include links to multiple resources, write a longer outline, annotate your outline, etc., but at some point, you need to start creating content.

It is important to note that you should not be afraid to deviate from your original outlines if you think you have something that can add more value to the chapter. You'll find that you may need to take away chapters or add others in too. And that's fine and normal. Chapter outlining is all about making sure that you start out on the right foot.

In summary: you should, at the minimum, include a 1- to 2-sentence description of the chapter. If you want to go further, that's great! But don't be afraid to start. It's alright if the first draft isn't perfect. That's what editing is for.

Alert! Writing Recommendations

That being said, there are some pitfalls to look out for and some recommendations we have for beginning the actual writing of your book.

Rec 1: Don't Keep Repeating Yourself

This is one of those telltale signs that you haven't planned your book out properly. You may have 30 different topics to talk about, but they can (and probably will) intersect with each other at some level because they're a part of the same overall topic. That's fine, and it's even good to repeat yourself a few times if it's an important theme or concept of the book. But don't take it too far.

When you find yourself using the same diagrams in separate chapters to explain the same thing—you know you've gone too far.

When you find yourself trying to phrase something in one chapter a different way so that the reader won't think you're repeating yourself—you've gone too far.

Again, don't repeat yourself.

Unless it's really important that a reader remembers something, it does not bear repeating.

It doesn't make for an engaging read if your readers finish the book and end up thinking, "I feel like that could have been said in 30 pages," so try hard not to put your readers through that.

Rec 2: Write the Last Chapter First

The first chapter you should write should be the last chapter.

Why?

Because you need to know where everything is leading to. Too many novels have bad endings because the writer got too caught up in the moment without thinking about the ending. If you don't know how things are going to shake out, it's easy to get off-track and start rambling.

For most people's purposes, your final chapter should probably be a call-to-action: "Now that you know this, this is what you should do now . . . ".

If you've spent the entire book telling a reader about how marketing will benefit their business and how best to leverage it, you've made them see you as an authority. In the final chapter, your call-to-action might be: "Hire me to improve your marketing plan", or "Hire me to create your marketing plan".

You may have somewhere else to take the reader after this, so your call-to-action might be: "Would you like to know about this?" and then you take them to one of your online courses, get them to create a login, and capture their email address.

Or very simply, your call-to-action could be: "Visit my author website at www.johnnorth.com.au".

It doesn't matter what it is, so long as you're asking your readers to do something after they finish your book. Always keep this ultimate call-to-action that your book ends with in mind when you are creating the content for the rest of your book. If you want them to learn more about *something* after they finish the book, then introduce the concept briefly in the final chapter, but don't explain it in detail. The point is to get them to do something in that final chapter that involves contacting you or learning more about your offerings.

REC 3: IMPROVE YOUR CHAPTER TITLES

Your chapter titles should:

- Briefly explain what the chapter is about
- Get your audience interested in the topic
- Not be more than 10 words total

It's okay to have boring chapter titles. Not every chapter title has to be exciting. But all of your titles should, on some level, fulfill the three conditions above.

You should be able to tell from the title what the chapter is going to entail, and it should be framed in an interesting way, if possible.

You don't want your readers to have to look through a table of contents that is three pages long, purely because of the obscene length of all the chapter titles. Each title should not be longer than your opening sentence. Two to four words per title is about right.

Some chapter titles might be as long as 10 words, but if you're going that far regularly, you may need to rethink the titles.

Sometimes chapter titles are too complex, and it would be better to simplify them for easier reading. This applies more to the less important chapters. For instance, the original chapter title for this chapter was "How to Write Chapter Outlines". It's already obvious that you're going to be writing chapter outlines in a book about writing books, so that part wasn't necessary, and it was cut to make the chapter title shorter and super easy and fast to read: "Chapter Outlines".

Improving your chapter titles as we've described here is a good exercise to do periodically, especially right after you've finished the first draft of your book.

Rapid Content Creation Strategies

Now that we've set the groundwork, it's time to start filling out your chapters with content. Our goal right now is for you to get as many words and ideas into the book as possible. If you blog regularly, you can easily repurpose that content for your book. Otherwise, you may be able to take content from presentations you've done. For now, insert that content into relevant chapters to refine and expand on later.

Rapid content creation is about pulling as much ready-made content into your book as possible so that you can focus on the chapters that you haven't spoken or written about before.

How to Get Content Quickly for Your Book

There will likely be chapters where you don't already have any content to use. That's okay. There are several easy ways to generate new content for your book that don't require much work.

Daily notes: every day, in your business, you are doing the work that you're talking about in your book. Write down ideas, tips, steps, and advice you give throughout your work week. Jot it down in a notebook, or record your conference calls. And when you're working on the book, look at these notes or listen to your recordings, and write it down.

The interview: have you interviewed an expert in the field you're talking about in your book? If you haven't, you should.

You can transcribe that interview and use it as a chapter. It's a quick, easy, and effective way to add value to your book. It's also a nice change of pace for readers from the preceding "how-to" chapters.

In fact, there are entire books that are made up of interviews with experts. This may be an avenue to consider when trying to get content for your book.

However, be careful. It's very easy to put other people on a pedestal when you should be establishing your own authority. One or two of these interviews is a good idea, but you should also have your own content, so readers will look to you as an expert.

The lesson: another great way to produce content is to write a chapter like a lesson. Teach your readers how to do something; for example, how to set up a successful email marketing campaign. Talk about how what you're teaching has benefited you and the ways it has benefitted you, and then write out the steps. Include some action steps at the end of the chapter for the reader to get started right now. For example, ask them to write out what they want their emails to push the people who've subscribed to their mailing list to do. You will probably have a number of these chapters.

The microphone method: otherwise, you could simply speak your book into a microphone. Talk about your field of work, the things you do, how you do them, and what has best worked for you. Then simply get the audio transcribed using one of the many online services that exist, like Rev.com.

This works a lot better if you have someone—for example, a friend or colleague—with you asking you questions. This is especially good for creating introductory chapters to a section or talking about your own success with the methods you describe.

The best way to frame your book as a conversation between you and the reader is to actually have a conversation with someone and use that to generate content for your book.

Get the easy chapters out of the way at the start, or at least include some usable and relevant content inside of them to clean up later. Remember, it's just a first draft, so it can be quite raw.

It's the chapters that remain that you've never already created written or spoken content about—and there will very likely be a number of them—that you need to focus on.

The Actual Content Creation Process

The previous chapter, "Rapid Content Creation Strategies", was about repurposing your current and tried-and-true content and getting the easy content out of the way. This chapter is about creating new content from scratch.

This is the hard part, but there are a lot of ways to expedite the content creation process. There are also a number of things you should consider when you're creating new content for your book.

Plan It Out

The small plan that we put in place in "Chapter Outlines" will start to become very useful. Focus on what the big picture ideas of the chapter are. If you need to, expand on the outline and list all of the things you need and want to talk about within each given chapter. It's easy to find yourself in the middle of a chapter and not knowing where to go next— that's what the plan is for. You can always refer back to the outline if you're stuck.

Slow at Typing?

The average person types at no more than 40 words a minute. Your word count is likely 35,000 words or more. While you've probably managed to make up most of the content for your book with rapid content creation, the remaining chapters will still take a number of hours to finish.

If you're slow at typing and prone to mistakes, this can be very frustrating and distracting. You might lose a train of thought and be stranded in the middle of a sentence.

There are several ways to combat this:

- **Get faster at typing.** There are numerous sites online that allow you to practice typing and teach you how to type properly. A lot of people never learn how to type properly. They just peck at the keyboard until their hands have memorised a familiar position. Being able to type properly is a valuable skill that you can take anywhere, but it's especially helpful for writing.
- **Speak your content.** Set aside some time every day to record yourself speaking out the content for your book. The average speaking speed is around 125 to 150 words per minute, which is faster than a lot of people will ever be able to type, so you won't need to worry about losing your train of thought or your hands not being able to keep up with your mind. Later, you can transcribe your spoken content into your book. Alternatively, you can try using voice recognition software (but this will be finicky and generally not very accurate) or try using transcription services.

WEAVE IN ENGAGING STORIES

You probably shouldn't do this in every chapter, but generally, you can add a lot of value to the book if you talk about your own experiences, success stories, and anecdotes. Not only will the reader connect with you, but you are also proving to them that your methods have tangible results.

Stories are also great because you don't have to do any outside research. You only need to recount your own experiences. It's content that's generally easy to write and is very effective at engaging the reader.

However, when telling stories, you need to be cautious. If you are writing a business book, and your branding is not centered around you, as an individual, you probably shouldn't be writing in the first person singular, meaning using "I" and "me".

And the stories you're telling probably shouldn't be your own, but your business's stories, meaning your professional experiences with clients. It's easy for a reader to make assumptions about your ego if you exclusively talk about yourself. To avoid this, you could simply decide not to tell as many stories. Focus primarily on providing educational content to the reader, and refer more to "case studies" than personal experiences.

Use your clients as examples of successful implementations of strategies, as examples of outliers, and/or as examples of a poorly-implemented strategy.

Use "we", not "I", when you talk about your professional experiences. And avoid talking about your personal ones.

First Drafts Are Not Meant to Be Perfect

It's easy to be discouraged when writing the first draft of a chapter because you may know, in the back of your head, "This isn't good enough", "I can't publish this", or "That sentence is awkward and I have no idea how to fix it!"

However, do not worry. Everybody—even seasoned writers—are bound to have these thoughts. The nature of a first draft is not for it to be perfect; it is to get the chapter down on paper.

Editing is where all of these mistakes are cleaned up. The important thing—the only thing you have to worry about—is that the content is basically readable, and you're getting your point across accurately.

Don't edit as you go. There is a time and a place for it, and that isn't the first draft. Write the first sentence, and then move on. There is no need to make the first sentence sound great just yet. All you're really doing is transcribing your ideas onto the page in their purest form.

It's okay to get a little discouraged. But remember, that's what editing is for. Push through and get it done.

Do Your Research

If you are creating a book in a field where there are several published books already, it's a great idea to look at their content and take inspiration from it. Look at the things they talk about, and provide your own take on the same topics in your book.

Of course, this doesn't just apply to books alone. Look at blogs, interviews, Wikipedia pages, and whatever is relevant to make sure that your book's content reflects popular topics and questions within the relevant field.

Additionally, you should also do research for the chapters you've already filled out via rapid content creation to add value to them. Verify the facts, but also look for statistics. If you're talking about heart attacks being a major killer in the world, look for official statistics from organisations like the American Heart Association. You're asking the reader to reflect for a moment on the importance of a topic or the value of a strategy, so backing your argument with relevant statistics adds weight to your words.

DRAFTING AND EDITING

Even if you've never written a thing in your life, you've probably heard of writers piling up draft after draft of their work, simply trying to get the flow of the story right.

Now, generally speaking, this applies more to novels than non-fiction books because fiction writers have to worry about plot/character consistency, how satisfying an ending is, whether the opening is gripping enough for a reader, whether an antagonist is convincing or threatening, whether the tone is right, etc. Getting a work of fiction "right" can be very tough, and it's common for a writer to want to throw out their first draft the instant they finish it.

But writing a non-fiction book, especially a logic book, is much easier, for a few reasons:

- You know exactly how and where you want to end your book, and where all the content in your book is ultimately going to lead to.
- It's often expected that you write in plain English, not the overblown, overdramatic, and over-written purple prose that literature is so often associated with.
- If you're writing a legacy book, you're essentially recounting all the details about something you know more intimately than anything else: yourself. There's no need to go out and research obscure facts in order to reproduce a convincing scene because you've lived those experiences first-hand.

It's precisely because non-fiction books are easier to plan and easier to write that they don't require nearly the comic amount of drafts fiction books are thought to have, but that doesn't mean they don't need editing. The very first draft of anything is rarely good. Especially if you're transferring content from one medium (a live speaking event) to another (a paper book). Repurposing that content means re-writing it to read well in print.

Editing does not just mean spell-checking and grammar-checking your manuscript for proper, readable English. That's the very first step of an editing job. And in some cases, making your manuscript read better means breaking some of those strict rules.

EDITING GOALS

When editing a manuscript, an editor usually has a few goals in mind.

The first goal is editing for understanding. This means making sure that a reader (specifically the target market) can understand what you've written. If you're writing for mathematicians, and only mathematicians, then it's perfectly alright to introduce vectors, matrices, and whatever advanced mathematical concept that any mathematician worth their salt should understand without any explanation whatsoever. On the other hand, if you're writing for beginners, it's definitely worth revising your work for better understanding.

It's common that the writer doesn't realise what they've written doesn't make any sense to the average reader, even after re-reading their work! The reason: you already know what you meant by the words you used, so it's easy for your brain to skip the words and go straight to the intention. This is especially true the closer you are to your work.

It's generally recommended that after you finish a chapter, or your entire book, you let it sit for a week or so and come back to it for the editing sweep. This is so that you can gain as much distance as you can from the mindset you were in when you originally wrote that chapter or that book.

Editing sooner than that is unproductive, or more often than not—*counterproductive*. This is why most writers do not edit their own work; at least not with the final edit. They hire an editor to do that for them.

The second goal is maintaining a consistent perspective. Did you know that most non-fiction books, specifically the business- and sales-oriented ones, are written predominately in the second-person perspective, meaning 'you'? This means that they address the reader personally, as if the reader has a stake in the conversation and the writer wants them to engage directly with the content of the book.

On the other side of the fence, almost no fiction books are written in the second-person perspective. Most of them are written in the third-person perspective—"he", "him", "she", "her", "it", "they", "them"—as if the reader is an outsider looking in on the story. The rest of fiction books are written in the first-person perspective—"I" and "me"—where the protagonist/ main character speaks about themselves, but (usually) without being cognizant of the reader.

There is, however, one type of fiction book that is written in the second-person perspective: *Choose Your Own Adventure* books. These books involve the reader (the "you") in the story by asking them (or "you") to make decisions that lead them (or "you") to what feels like their ("your") own ending.

And when you think about it, these business-oriented books that also use the second person are doing much the same thing. They're providing the reader ("you") with information in order to make a decision at the end on whether the business is worth hiring or not to achieve their ("your") personal goals.

That's the reasoning behind why so many business books find the second-person perspective ("you") to be much more powerful than the first- or third- person perspective.

This is why we recommend that you write your book mostly in second-person perspective. An editor will be focused on maintaining that perspective all throughout your book, in case you suddenly slip into first or third person without realising it.

The third goal is maintaining a consistent tone. Especially if you are writing a hybrid of a legacy and logic book, you may find that your book suffers from tone whiplash. One paragraph, the tone could be formal and written from a business perspective, and the next, the tone is casual and personal, and right back around again.

It's the editor's job to decide how to bridge the two tones appropriately within the same chapter or if one of those paragraphs even belongs in that chapter. It's perfectly okay to have shifting tones in your book, but they need to be appropriate and make sense before they can be put into action. Otherwise, they are liable to confuse and disorient readers.

The important thing to realise about all of these goals is that the editor will attempt to achieve these goals with your book based on their own biases and editing experience about what is "right", or what "feels right". This will not necessarily line up with your own goals for your book, so you need to carefully read the changes made to decide whether they are valuable edits or not. Ultimately, it's up to you whether you think your book would benefit from those changes.

With that said …

When you're self-publishing, your editor offers feedback to improve your work. When you're working with a traditional publisher, your editor is a gatekeeper that will alter your work in accordance with the publisher's own goals and sensibilities.

At Evolve Global Publishing, our only concern is giving your manuscript the best feedback possible through our editors. Our goal is opening the doors to publishing platforms, not closing them when we don't agree with what you've written. If you want to find out more about our editing services, visit: evolveglobalpublishing.com.

STEP 3: PUBLISHING YOUR BOOK

Now that your book is ready to publish, you need to perform specific tasks to make sure that your book is available in as many places as possible.

We cover all the necessary topics, including:

- An ISBN—what is it?!
- Book types
- Book formatting
- The publishing process
- Traditional publishers—what about them?
- Making a profit

These steps are vital to ensure your book is professionally completed, so you can start to achieve the goals we talked about in the early chapters.

ISBNs

Have you purchased ISBNs for your book?

This question can open a can of worms!

Why?

There are several ways of getting ISBNs, but it's very easy to get lost. Nearly every new author gets very confused about this topic. One reason it can be confusing is that some ISBNs are free while others cost hundreds of dollars. Let's look into ISBNs a bit more.

An ISBN is essentially a unique barcode issued per type of book (e.g., printed book, hardcover book, eBook). In other words, your book will have a different ISBN for its paperback edition than it will for its hardcover edition.

Here's what Wikipedia has to say about ISBNs: *"The International Standard Book Number is a numeric commercial book identifier which is intended to be unique. Publishers purchase ISBNs from an affiliate of the International ISBN Agency. An ISBN is assigned to each edition and variation of a book."*

You can search any ISBN via https://isbnsearch.org/

ACQUIRING YOUR ISBNS

There are a few places online where you can buy ISBNs, and prices can vary significantly. In addition, many online platforms (such as Amazon) provide free ISBNs.

Essentially, you can purchase an ISBN two ways:

1. Direct from the main ISBN suppliers, such as Thorpe-Bowker
2. Indirect from bulk ISBN agents

The general difference is that bulk ISBN agents can pre-register the "imprint name". An **imprint** of a publisher is a trade name under which it publishes a work. This is what Amazon does when they provide you with a free one.

Most authors choose option 1 because they want their name to appear as the publisher. Historically, we have used bulk buy agents because they are a lot cheaper and generally achieve the same result. We usually take the free ones from Amazon and buy ISBNs for all other platforms. You don't need an ISBN for Amazon Kindle, as they supply their own identification code: an ASIN.

The ONLY time your ISBN will be relevant is if your book finds its way to a bookstore because they need the barcode to identify it. Otherwise, it is largely useless if you print and sell your own books, but it does help make it look official, whether it is one acquired by option 1 or 2.

LAYOUT AND FORMATTING

Laying out and formatting a book is something that too many authors fail to consider. The absolute biggest mistake that almost every green author makes is writing their book entirely in Microsoft Word. A Word document has to be completely stripped of all special formatting in order to be useable for an interior (i.e., the file that contains all of the text, images, etc., for the inside of your book). The longer the book, the more man hours it takes to transfer all of the content from a Word document into our proprietary program, EvolveBookPublisher. com, to be ready for publishing.

The other big downside is that often, all of the special formatting an author does for their book in Word will have to be dumbed down significantly to be simpler and more parseable for an eBook file to understand and render properly. Even for print books, special formatting has to be stripped down to plain text to avoid weird formatting errors that Word creates and then improve the formatting in the layout process. This often results in a lot of wasted effort.

It is also very difficult to create useable .PDF Interior files for a print interior from Word. Laying out a book for print is a tedious and involved process that usually takes a few days to complete properly.

Professionals use Adobe InDesign to lay out a book. If an author wants to do this themselves, they will probably need to undertake a few hours of training if they aren't familiar with the program. Free tutorials are available online, particularly on YouTube, but if you want to do it right, you'll want to learn from a more professional source, such as PluralSight.

You do not want to end up missing small details or making small mistakes because you had never thought about how a book should be properly formatted before. For example, you do not indent the first line of every paragraph in the book; the very first paragraph under each chapter heading is not indented.

HERE ARE SOME COMMON MISTAKES AND FORMATTING RULES THAT MIGHT TRIP YOU UP:

- Indent the first line of every paragraph except the first one.
- If you have links in your paperback book, leave them unstyled, meaning in plain text with no hyperlink embedded in them. Make them clickable in your eBook version, meaning embed them with a hyperlink.
- Make sure you have at least 5 lines below a headline inside a chapter. Don't start a headline on the last line of the page; it's confusing for the reader and looks unprofessional.
- Always start a new chapter on a new page.
- Always start a new chapter on either the right or left page of the book. Typically, most books start chapters on the right page of the book, but the most important thing is consistency. Make sure that every chapter starts on the left page, or every chapter starts on the right page. This makes it both easier to flip through quickly and offers a cleaner, more standard design.
- Every book needs a copyright page, and the font size should be shrunken down enough so it fits on one page (unless your copyright details are especially lengthy). This is where your ISBNs go.
- The very first page of your book should contain your book title (in the same font as the front cover) and the author name below it. This is the title page.
- Right before the table of contents but after the copyright and title page, you should include any dedications you have.

- You can either locate your table of contents directly after these three pages or after the rest of the **front matter (content that precedes the main body of the book)**. If your other front matter (acknowledgments, introduction, foreword, preface, etc.) is short enough, then you can include the table of contents after the front matter. This is because you don't want the table of contents to be the first thing the reader sees, but you also don't want them to dig through 20 pages to find it. Ten pages of the front matter before the table of contents is about the limit.

Keep in mind that these are just some commonsense formatting rules; this not an exhaustive list of requirements or guidelines. If you are going to format your own book, you will have to make sure it conforms to as many of these as possible.

If you don't have the time to learn a new program, it's easier and often more accurate just to pay a professional to lay out your book for you.

WE OFFER LAYOUT AND FORMATTING SERVICES AT EVOLVEGLOBALPUBLISHING.COM.

Book Types

Generally speaking, there are three mediums you can get your book published in:

Paperback and Hardcover

The paper book is the most traditional medium that you can and should get your book published in. Everybody knows and recognises it as the industry standard, and automatically views it as professional; even if the cover is lacking.

Paper books have more customisation options than eBooks or audiobooks. You can change the colour of the interior paper. You can change the size of the book (a children's book might be very rectangular, for instance, while a normal book would be closer to 6x9. Fantasy novels tend to be very big). You can change the feel of the book from matte to glossy, or even add embossing. You can choose to publish it in economical paperback, or a collector's edition hardcover version. You can customise or add numerous other features with a paper book. It's the flagship form you want your book to be in.

EBOOK

Digital books are a relatively new paradigm that has been hit-or-miss with a lot of readers. It's convenient to carry around a Stephen King tome in your pocket, but some readers believe that it's a lot less immersive and more damaging to the eyes than having a book you can tangibly feel. A great benefit to having an eBook is that you can make free updates to the book without forcing readers to buy a second edition. Readers will always have the best version of your book.

However, eBooks are also viewed as less valuable than print books, simply because readers think that anybody can write them. And, the truth is, there are many more eBooks than there are print books, and this is because there is no barrier to entry. Anyone can write and publish their own eBook, which is great for aspiring writers, but not so good for critical readers. This is why an eBook is a good format to have your book published in (it's very convenient and cheap to buy), but it shouldn't be the only one.

Audiobook

Finally, the hardest but most interesting format to get your book published in is as an audiobook. Audiobooks are not a format that just anybody can get their book published in easily. It's a lot of work, and it can take a number of weeks for somebody to finish voicing your book.

However, the final result is great for readers who don't have much idle time to flip through a book. They can listen to it while they're driving to work or before bed. It also makes it more accessible to blind or partially blind readers, while deaf or partially deaf readers can read the paperback/eBook editions.

An audiobook is something you should only consider doing after you have already published your book in print and digitally because the production time scale is much higher than the previous two. Audiobooks are not very common, especially among the self-published, so it is a nice bonus option for readers to have.

Which Format to Choose?

Ideally, you would want to get your book published in all of these formats in order to make it as available as possible to as many people as possible. However, this takes a lot of time and effort, and audiobooks, in particular, will force you to reach for your wallet. It is far easier to publish your book in one format first and then republish it in other formats.

And if you are only going to publish your book in one format, it should be in paperback and/or hardcover. As already mentioned, there is a school of thought that dismisses eBooks as "not real books".

A paper book is traditional, respected, and professional. An eBook is convenient. And knowing there is an audiobook version available boosts the perceived quality of your book (because of how hard it is to produce one) before a reader even opens the book. An audiobook is the ultimate love letter; it really emphasises how much of a labour of love your book was.

Getting your book published in paperback can be quick and easy, or hard and time-consuming, depending on the service that you choose to use. Amazon is the quickest and easiest option available, but it doesn't provide as many options as a service like IngramSpark does. Amazon also doesn't allow you to create a hardcover print book. If you want to publish a hardcover edition, IngramSpark offers a multitude of options, but it is more difficult to set up with them than with Amazon.

Next, you want to get an eBook version of your book published. This can be accomplished easily in Amazon. They accept .mobi and .epub file formats. Of the two, .epub is the format you should use for your published eBook. Generally speaking, .mobi is a file format designed for previewing your eBook.

IngramSpark has an option to publish your eBook, but you have very little control over your book when using them because you cannot allocate categories (which reduces the chances of your book being found by Amazon's search engine greatly). If you want to update your pricing (e.g., for a special event; a one-time offer, etc.), it can be slow to update, as opposed to Amazon, which usually updates it within a few hours.

Additionally, you should know too that Amazon Sales Reporting isn't in real-time; it can take up to 30 days before you see the sales reports.

If this all sounds a bit confusing, that's because it is. You can create your eBook easily through EvolveBookPublisher.com without having to worry about all of the technical details. The benefit of this program is that you can create a digital book on the fly (and publish it on Amazon) and review it and make any changes to prepare to get your book formatted for print.

Lastly—and you should really only worry about this after you've already published your book in the previous formats and finished making any major changes—you can republish your book as an audiobook. The cheapest (not necessarily the easiest) way to do this is to record it yourself. You will need professional audio recording devices, a sound-proofed area that is optimal for recording (a recording studio), and many, many hours to record your book.

If you don't have the time or the inclination, Evolve Global Publishing offers a complete done-for-you service based on price-per-word where a professional voice-over artist (male or female) can record your book and create professionally-engineered audio files, which can be accepted by all the major audiobook platforms, such as Audible, Nook Audiobooks (Barnes & Nobles' audiobook platform), Scribd, etc.

IF YOU WANT TO FIND OUT MORE, VISIT EvolveGlobalPublishing.com.

WHY SHOULDN'T YOU PUBLISH WITH A TRADITIONAL PUBLISHER?

Publishing a book is a big headache for many writers who already have the book done, but can't find anybody to publish it for them. Traditional book publishers will want to read through, edit, and sometimes re-work your book if they think it's a good fit for them. But often, all writers get from a traditional publisher is a letter of rejection saying: "This manuscript is not a good fit for our publishing house at this time".

It's a lot of trouble to get a traditional publisher to want to publish your book, but once your foot is in the door, it's smooth sailing from there, right?

The reason publishers are so sought after is because they have a huge network of retailers, producers, and celebrities that they can promote your book through. But you will also find that a publisher wants to know what your "platform" is like. What they mean—as previously discussed—is they want the answers to these questions: how many social media followers do you have? How many email addresses and famous connections do you have?

This is why they are called "publishers" and not "marketers". Their main job is to publish your book to the general market. They still expect you to promote it for future sales. But they do all the legwork and all the things that you can't do alone. They're a very valuable agent in the book publishing industry. Naturally, traditional publishing houses certainly think so too, which is why they commonly offer a 70-30 cut of the profits their way.

Having the opportunity to sell your book on a popular and respected platform, like the Amazon Marketplace, is often worth the profit cut because you will make sales that you never would have been able to otherwise on your own website.

The profit cut for your publisher, however, often isn't as worth it, because they will commonly want to stake a claim on your book by buying the intellectual property off you, meaning that you no longer have the right to sell your own book anywhere else—because you no longer own the book. And they still only cut you in on 30% of the profits.

Essentially, the traditional publisher is buying the rights off of you for them to be able to do whatever they want with your book and cutting you in on a percentage of the profits. While you do get to utilise their connections, sell it in popular bookstores like Barnes & Noble, and benefit from all of the marketing that they do for your book, you are now bound to the publisher.

That is, of course, if they do end up doing all that marketing for your book. Typically, they'll get your book in the new releases section in Barnes & Noble and maybe run a few light promotions on TV networks, but you probably aren't getting as much of a leg up as you think you're getting.

At the same time, because the publisher now has full rights to your content, they may also restrict you from using that content elsewhere, for example, in an online course.

One of the biggest hurdles to overcome, even if you do get accepted by a publisher, is timing. Publishers typically take anywhere from 12 to 18 months to publish your book. That's a long time for most entrepreneurs, and you could have easily missed the boat by the time your book is available to the marketplace. Traditional publishers work on their schedule, not yours.

Evolve Global Publishing does not stake a claim on your book. We offer to edit and create a cover for your book, and push it out to as many platforms as possible. You are not bound to us; you can take your book wherever you want after the process is done. We also offer a 30-70 cut—your way.

Why Should You Self-Publish Your Book?

Self-publishing is a very popular way of publishing books. The degree of success varies from book to book. A lot of self-published books end up lost and forgotten while others become international phenomenons; think of the highly-repeated success story from the author of *Fifty Shades of Grey*. The work originally started as fanfiction for another incredibly popular series, *Twilight*. When forced to remove it from the site for its sexual content, the writer decided to remove all the references to *Twilight* and republished it on her website as an eBook. This initially self-published book became such a big hit that it was adapted into a film.

So, certainly, there is nothing preventing a self-published book from becoming a global phenomenon. However, there is a lot more work in self-publishing than in other avenues. Unless you have a sizable following already and powerful marketing resources at your disposal, it is unlikely that your book will become incredibly successful.

As long as you level your expectations, self-publishing is a great way to publish your book, if you do it right!

There are some huge benefits to being self-published:

- **There is no one to tell you what to do.** You have the final say on what you want to include in your book and how you want to say it.
- **You get all the royalties.** If you publish your book with a traditional publisher, you would likely end up with 30% of the profits. If you self-publish your book, you get all the profits—unless the platform you're publishing your book on wants a reasonable cut of the profits too.

- **You get to choose who you want to work with.** Once you've signed the contract with a traditional publisher, it's their editor that checks and re-writes your work to the publisher's sensibilities. If you don't like the way it's edited, often it's just too bad. As a self-published author, you can do your editing yourself, or you can hire whoever you want online to do your editing for you. Creating and refining the cover is a similar situation. In self-publishing, the cover is whatever you want it to be. You are the one in control.
- **It's easier.** Trying to sell your book rights to a traditional publisher is notoriously difficult. You can spend months pedaling it to every traditional publisher in town, and all you get back is: "This isn't a good fit for our publishing house". This wastes a lot of time, and when you do find a publisher that wants your work, they may bring out a laundry list of restrictions and compromises that you have to agree to before they accept it.
- **It's faster.** Publishing houses can take 6 to 18 months to edit, re-edit, re-edit, create a cover, set up distribution channels, promote, and finally release your book. Self-publishing your book can be done in a week or less. If you want to get your book done, and get it done now, self-publishing is the fastest way to do it.

However, there are also a number of pitfalls you can fall into with self-publishing. Book publishing is an involved process with a lot of over-complicated steps and hoops to jump through, so it's easy to get to a point where all you want to do is get it done—not get it done properly. It's also easy to get it wrong.

Common Errors

These are some of the mistakes we see self-published authors make:

Designing Your Own Cover

This is probably the absolute worst mistake a self-published author can make because a bad cover means a bad first impression. We talked about this briefly in "Designing an Awesome Cover", but it's worth revisiting. Often, you can easily tell a self-published book from a traditionally published book just from its cover. A self-published book's cover "just doesn't look right". This applies especially to fiction books because they often feature their main characters on the cover, but non-fiction books are not immune.

Why is this?

It's because the images on the cover don't look "official". This is often a result of using stock images poorly. Your main character should not be represented by the first image result for "bare-chested man" on iStockPhoto. Even when the images are non-specific, it still looks wrong. Maybe the images don't blend properly, the title is hard to read, the image quality is fuzzy, or the font is unprofessional or unreadable.

Most authors who design their own covers do not design very good covers. Most author's friends do not design very good covers. It's cheap, easy, and in-house to create your own cover, but a good first impression is worth the money for a proper cover design. This is one cost you should absolutely not be frugal about.

Refer back to the "Designing an Awesome Cover" chapter for more information on this crucial element of your book.

USING A PRE-MADE COVER

This is debatably worse than designing your own cover poorly. If you pay for and use a pre-made cover, it is very likely that there are other authors out there using the same cover as you. It looks very unprofessional when two books look essentially the same with different wording. While it may not have been cheap to obtain a pre-made cover, it definitely looks cheap to the eyes of a potential reader when they see three identical covers in the "related" section on Amazon.

Using cover templates, however, is not a bad idea. It's a good place to start, but you should alter it to suit your needs. Change the images, change the font, and change the colour scheme. A cover template will likely not be everything you want your cover to look like, so you will end up making a number of changes to it. However, it's sometimes easier to start designing a cover from a template if it is similar enough to what you want.

You can hand over this mockup cover design to a professional designer who will re-create it to your specifications.

DOING A BAD EDITING JOB

Because most self-published authors are conscious about cost, it's easy to think you can get away with doing your editing yourself if you think you're a good enough writer. Sometimes authors don't even think about editing and publish the book the moment they finish it. This is certain: your first draft is going to be riddled with typos, awkward sentence structure, incorrect use of grammar, and an overall unpolished nature. You should do at least one editing pass for your work—this will fix most of these issues if done properly.

You should also get a professional editor to proof your work, no matter how good a writer you are. You need to make sure that others understand what you've written. It may seem obvious to you because you're the one who wrote it, but because you're so close to the work, there are some things you just can't see.

Refer back to the "Drafting and Editing" chapter for more detail on editing.

Publishing Your Book Only on Your Own Site

You should publish your book everywhere. The number of readers that buy books directly from the author's website is less compared to the number of readers that buy on Amazon, Book Depository, BookTopia, etc. This is especially true if you only accept Stripe payments as opposed to PayPal. Many readers will simply not enter their details on any other site than Amazon.

If your book is only available on your own site, you are inconveniencing potential readers because of the extra hoops they have to jump through in order to buy a book on an unfamiliar site. If your book is on Amazon and a number of other popular online bookstores, it increases the credibility of your book. It also increases your visibility and the possibility of organic sales.

It can, however, be difficult to set up accounts and books on these sites, so it is understandable why some self-published authors don't do it. However, you shouldn't be one of them! You should make your book available as broadly as possible.

Is It Worth the Effort?

Self-publishing your book allows you to have greater control over the content and distribution of your book, but precisely because of that, it can be easy to make mistakes. A traditional book publisher does all of the leg work for you and pays you up-front even if the book does poorly. Using a traditional publisher that is experienced with these issues can save you a lot of trouble, and it may be worth only getting 30% of the royalties.

But self-publishing is still a great way to publish your book if you can dedicate the time and energy to doing it properly. A lot of the work is on you, and it's up to you to say what is good enough. You have to hire editors and cover designers, set up your books on Amazon and other popular online bookstores, and you have to market your book. If you can handle doing those things, self-publishing may be the right choice for you—especially if you want to get your book published quickly.

However, there is one more option for publishing your book: hybrid publishers.

WHAT ABOUT HYBRID PUBLISHING?

Most people have heard about traditional publishers and self-publishing, but hybrid publishers aren't as widely known about. Essentially, the idea is that a hybrid publisher takes cues from self-publishing and traditional publishing and combines the two in a way that greatly benefits authors. Instead of selling your rights to a traditional publisher, you pay a hybrid publisher a set fee to edit, design a cover, and/or distribute your book to as many channels as possible (typically more than are available as a self-published author).

Evolve Global Publishing is a hybrid publisher. We don't stake a claim on authors' books; we are an intermediary for editing, designing covers, and publishing your book. We also offer a 70-30 cut, where you get the bigger slice of the pie.

The biggest benefit of working with hybrid publishers is that you have a similar level of control to self-publishing, but your level of responsibility and the amount of work you do is considerably less. Hybrid publishers need to publish books to a certain degree of quality, so will work to make sure that the process is properly done. Hybrid publishers are also far less selective about what authors they take on, so you won't usually have to worry about being rejected.

Depending on the publisher, they may also offer marketing services for after the book is published to ensure that both parties get a good return on investment.

Choosing a hybrid publisher just to publish a book that you've worked on yourself up until this point may be a good idea, as well. There is a certain amount of bias directed toward self-published authors from readers; for example, that they are unprofessional. This, of course, is an unfair judgment to make based solely on an author publishing their book themselves, but using a hybrid publisher avoids the situation regardless.

WHEN SHOULD YOU WORK WITH A HYBRID PUBLISHER?

To work with a hybrid publisher, you will need to be able to pay them. If you aren't willing to spend money on your book, self-publishing is a better option. Hybrid publishers are also a good option when you don't have time or skill to do all of the work your book needs to be done to get it published. You can go to a hybrid publisher when you've finished your manuscript and need editing services, a cover, and to be published, or you can approach them at a later stage, where the only thing you need is to be published; so it's flexible.

Evolve Global Publishing offers to work with you to create, edit, publish, and promote your book. If all you have is an idea and the desire to create a book, we can take you through the entire process, from start to finish. We offer cover design services, editing services, promotional services, and we offer to work with you to help you create your book.

Making a Profit

As mentioned in the "Creating" section, the cost of printing (i.e., how much an individual copy of your book will cost to print) is based on several major factors:

1. **The number of images in your book**—images require much more toner to print than text.
2. **Whether you want to print your book in colour**—your book can double in price depending on how many images you have.
3. **The number of pages in your book**—a book with 108 pages is going to be a lot cheaper to print than a book with 116 pages.
4. **The type of book you are printing: paperback or hardcover**—hardcover versions require much more high-quality materials to make; paperbacks are more economical for both you and your reader.
5. **The number of books you are printing at once: bulk or small numbers**—most printers are willing to provide a discount for bulk orders.

Naturally, the cost of printing will affect how much profit you make on each book. The price of your book should never be less than the cost of printing; otherwise, you will be losing money on each book you print. Your profit will also be affected by the platform you are selling your book on. Bookstores, for instance, will take a cut of the profits for providing an opportunity to sell to their customers. Many traditional publishers will also take a cut of the profits, as well. Profit cuts are almost impossible to avoid unless you publish your book entirely by yourself and sell it through your own platform.

Keep in mind that you do not have to make a direct profit from your book for it to be considered a success. One of the most powerful ways you can use your book to create opportunities for a greater profit down the line is by capitalising your book as a source of credibility and reputation.

You have to consider what is more important to you: **earning direct profit from your book** or **getting your book into the hands of as many people as possible**. This will be covered in greater detail in a later chapter of the book.

However, if you want to maximise the profit you make from your book itself while still keeping the price reasonable and affordable for readers, there are a few things you can do:

1. **Print your book in black and white.** Unless you have a lot of diagrams that would be next to unreadable in black and white, there isn't really any reason to publish your book in colour anyway. Colour is the single biggest cost factor that can drive your cost of printing up or down.

2. **Remove some images.** Ask yourself how many of those images are really benefiting your book. It's often the case that there are a few too many images in the book for its own good.

    Does it complement or clarify an argument you are making? How many images are there in each chapter of your book? Does it break the reader's focus on what you're saying to have a new image after only a few paragraphs of text?

3. **Increase the price.** Ideally, you want your hardcover version to be the definitive edition of your book. You want to be making the biggest profit on your hardcover edition while keeping the paperback economical. But if you do want to make a reasonable profit on the paperback too, you can sell it for $19.95 instead of $12.95. Your eBook costs virtually nothing to distribute, so you can

price it anywhere from $0.99 to $9.95, and readers still consider it a reasonable purchase.

If you're wondering what the ideal price you should have for each edition of your book, this is covered in extensive detail in the next section.

STEP 4:
PROMOTING
YOUR BOOK

Your book should now be finally completed, but no one knows about it yet. It's time to get your marketing hat on and start working on getting your message out to your market.

We talk about why a best-selling book can be the kick-start to your marketing campaign. You will also need some assets in place, like an author website and perhaps a book selling funnel.

Other topics include:

- Pricing your book
- Creating a launch campaign
- Generating Leads
- Getting Reviews
- Harnessing Social media
- Creating an author website
- Creating a book marketing plan

We have a lot of work to do, so let's get started immediately!

PRICING

There isn't a perfect price for your book. However, it is important that the thought process that goes into pricing the various editions of your book is sound and logical. You have to understand why people buy products at high prices and why they refuse to buy them at low prices—or even refuse to take them for free.

What sort of book are you selling?

Lead Generation: your book should be priced low at 99 cents for Kindle and below $20 for the paperback.

Authority: your book should be priced at $2.99 to $4.99 for Kindle, and $21.95 to $29.95 for paperback.

Profit Source: your book should be priced at $4.99 to $9.99 for Kindle, and $21.95 and above for paperback.

One area to consider is to have a hardcover book as well as a paperback. Not only can you charge a lot more for it, but this also gives you another unique listing of your book on all your platforms. We have found that, out of 100 buyers of your paperback, around 20 to 30% will opt for the hardcover version. This means more profits from the sale of your book.

Prices are not set in stone and can be easily changed on most platforms. But some can take a few months to reflect the price changes you've made. Amazon usually takes less than 72 hours to publish changes.

Try not to put a price on your printed book's barcode (ISBN). In most cases, bookstores will want their own price. Additionally, it could be harder to sell if you decided to increase your price, but your older books were valued at a lower price due to a price printed on your book's ISBN.

The other factor to consider is to whether you should price the book differently depending on the platform that sells it. Amazon is the major player for book sales, but other platforms like Apple, Kobo, Google Books, and Barnes & Noble also have a place in the overall marketing of the book. Your sales on these other platforms will likely be a lot lower than on Amazon. Accordingly, you should think about whether you should have consistent pricing on all platforms, or have a unique price for each platform to attract more sales or make more royalties given the particular clientele or nature of the platform.

So, prior to uploading and publishing your book, make sure you decide on your pricing. Changing it later could be challenging or confusing to your market.

Of course, if you want to initially launch your book to get best-seller status, we recommend a price of 99 cents during the launch period to attract as many sales as possible.

International Best-Seller Campaign

As you may well know if you've visited a bookstore recently, the best-selling books are put at the front of the store and promoted above all of the other books. Getting your book to achieve best-seller status is the best thing that you can do for it because it opens so many doors. Once you have a best-selling book, you become a best-selling author. And once you have another best-selling book, you become a two-time best-selling author. The promotional power of a best-seller also extends to you, as an author.

Of course, it's one thing to admire the power behind a best-seller, and another thing for your book to become a best-seller. This chapter is meant to serve as a rough guide to turning your book into a best-seller on Amazon.

Before we can do that, however, you need to know what a "best-seller" actually means.

Best-Selling Book: this is a book that usually appears on some sort of top-selling list of books in a certain industry, store, or category. For our purposes, this refers to becoming the top-selling book in an Amazon category (i.e., selling more books in a certain timeframe than any other book in the category). And before you can do that, you have to choose the right categories.

Choosing the Best Categories for Your Book

All books, by default, are included in the overall parent category "Books", which means you are competing with every single book on the Amazon Marketplace (this is literally millions of books with dozens, if not hundreds more appearing daily).

To become a best-seller in this category, you would need to outsell every single book for sale on Amazon in a certain timeframe. This is incredibly difficult to do without a very powerful promotion, so it's a good idea to choose more than just one category.

Amazon currently allows you to choose up to 10 categories for your Kindle book as well as 10 more for your physical book. And this is an important point—you should be focusing on selling your Kindle book, not your paperback, hardcover, or audiobook because they don't have nearly as much reach as a digital book.

You will always sell more eBook copies than you do of physical or audiobook copies, simply because they are cheaper and are delivered instantly without any delivery fees.

Back to determining your book categories: think about your book. Is it a business book?

If so, you should choose relevant "children categories", which are categories that exist inside of the main "parent" category inside of the "Business" category. Try to choose, in addition to the main "Books" category, at least two relevant, specific categories. The more, the better.

If you choose relevant categories, you will be able to generate more sales organically. For example, when somebody is looking for a business book inside of the "small business" subcategory, they may find your book and decide to purchase it.

WHAT IS "BSR"?

This is a very important term in Amazon and means "Best Sellers Rank". On each book in Amazon, if you scroll to the "Product Details" area, you will see a list of categories and a number before it, e.g., #20. This means that this book is ranked #20 in sales for this category. You are looking to get as many #1 rankings as you can for your book on launch day.

Amazon shows a book's top three categories and will cycle through any others if it ranks higher. Categories are updated hourly for popular ones and can take up to 24 hours to update the less popular ones.

Setting Up a Launch Campaign

Because you need to make the bulk of the sales for your book within a certain timeframe in order for Amazon to label your book (and promote it) as a best-seller, you will need to set up a launch campaign, taking place within a 24-hour period. All of the sales that count toward your sales figures will be captured within that time period. Keep in mind the differences between time zones.

Essentially, what you are doing is telling your mailing list about your book and asking them to buy it within this time period. One great way to encourage purchases is by promising them something that they won't get if they order at any other time. This could be something like a poster, a companion guidebook to a topic you only briefly touch on, or a discount on your services, etc. Because it's limited, the perceived value increases; it will feel like they're missing out if they don't buy within that time period.

However, messaging your mailing list out of the blue about your new book without any kind of lead up to it will naturally lead to mixed results. Another issue is that because it's such a short timeframe, some people will simply miss the email, even if they're dedicated to following you. So, you should send a few emails in advance about your book to get your followers interested in it before you ask them to buy it. You should mention the release date in advance so that they aren't caught off-guard.

To maximise the amount of sales you get within this short time period, it's a good idea to create a Facebook Group dedicated to your upcoming book. You can get members excited about your book beforehand and prepare them for the date that your book is released. You should still send your mailing list that email, but you now have a second avenue to notify people who have proven that they are interested in buying your book. Some people may not check their emails for a day, but they will likely check Facebook several times a day, so it's a great place to host your launch group.

Also, the book that you are asking everyone to buy should be your Kindle book. You should set the price to 99 cents to encourage as many sales as possible. Asking people to buy your Kindle book for $2.99 or higher is likely to result in a sharp reduction in sales compared to a lower price.

Amazon does have file size limits for eBooks, currently around 2mb, so be careful your formatted digital book is not too big. In some cases, we have had to produce a cut-down-sized file and lower image quality to get it under the file size limit.

Setting up a great launch campaign is all about getting people interested in your book beforehand and capitalising on that excitement by surprising them with a limited item that they won't get at any other time.

To achieve a best-seller, you need to push people to purchase your book within that 24-hour period, and the best way to do that is to make it feel like they'll be missing out on something too if they miss that date.

What's an "International" Best-Seller?

The difference between a "best-seller" and an "international best-seller" is that your book ranked as the #1 book in multiple categories, in multiple countries. An international best-seller campaign requires more work to pull off, but it adds more credibility when you get the title.

When you publish your book on Amazon, make sure you choose all countries. Amazon has a separate marketplace for each country, and as a result, the categories for Amazon.co.uk (Britain) will be vastly different from Amazon.com, Amazon.ca (Canada), and Amazon.com.au (Australia). The UK has the least categories of the three, so it may be difficult to find specific, relevant categories in which to place your book. You will need to make enough sales on each separate marketplace in order to achieve a #1 in those categories, so you will need to change up your launch campaign strategy slightly.

Because you need to make a similar number of sales on multiple different marketplaces, that means that a segment of your followers will need to buy your book on amazon.co.uk, another segment will need to buy your book on amazon.com, and so on. This will be more difficult to do if most of your followers live in the US, as you can't reasonably ask somebody to buy your book twice if they have multiple Amazon accounts.

Instead, the best way to generate sales on multiple marketplaces is by including links to your book on all marketplaces in the email you send or the post you make. UK followers will use the .co.uk link to buy your book, Australian followers will use the .com.au link, and American followers will use the .com link.

One last thing, Asian countries are a bit of a challenge when promoting your book on Amazon. Countries such as China, Singapore, Malaysia, and Hong Kong won't let people buy Kindle books Amazon. But it will let them buy paperbacks! Why Amazon does this no-one is prepared to say, but we suspect it's due to piracy issues.

This is why an "international best-seller" is worth more than just a "best-seller". It's much harder to achieve.

WHAT IS A "HOT NEW RELEASE"?

We have seen people think they have a "best-seller" and in fact, it's actually a "hot new release". This is a totally separate ranking system that Amazon has, and often you will find this will rank first here before best-seller, and you will even find these achievements don't always line up with best-seller results either. We track both to really enhance the final campaign result.

So, for example:

#1 Best Seller x 20 categories in 4 Countries
#1 Hot New Release x 22 categories in 4 Countries

WHERE'S MY BADGE?

Something that has stumped a lot of authors who try for a best-seller on Amazon is that they aren't notified of when they receive #1 in a category.

They finish their campaign, not aware of whether they've actually achieved it or not. Sometimes Amazon will add a "Best Seller" badge to the top of the page when you do achieve this, but sometimes they won't. The only real indicator of whether you've achieved it or not is this section of the page, as seen in this screenshot:

Right below **"Amazon Best Sellers Rank"**, you will see the categories you chose for your book.

If they have "#1 in [category]", this means that you've achieved a #1. The orange badge that says "Best Seller", also pictured in the screenshot, does not necessarily appear even when you do achieve a #1 best-seller, so the absence of the badge does not mean you haven't achieved a best-seller.

Sometimes if you search your book in Amazon, it will display your best-seller badge with it. Make sure you take screenshots of as much of the categories and book page as you can for future proof. This is because the ranking could change an hour later.

Also, you will have to re-edit your cover once you achieve the best-seller to include your own best-seller badge on it, as Amazon will not do this either.

Once you finish the process, you now have the right to call yourself a best-selling author!

LEAD GENERATION

Your book is a great lead generation tool. Readers who are interested in doing something will seek out information. The best place to get reliable information easily is a book.

By that stage, when a reader picks up your book, you are already an expert in their mind. You know what you're doing.

Otherwise, you wouldn't have been able to write a book about it. By having published a book, you have positioned yourself as an expert in their mind.

So, how do you go from being a respected expert to being a valued business partner?

How do you get your reader to want to spend money with you to do the thing that you've taught in your book?

KNOW YOUR CUSTOMER

Your customer is most likely not the inspired, motivated go-getter who is willing (and able) to do everything themselves.

Your customer is most likely not broke, unmotivated, and unwilling to pay you, but may want to "pick your brain" .

Your customer is most likely not willing or able to implement the steps, strategies, tips, or advice you've oultined in your book.

Your customer wants help. Your customer can't do these things themselves. Your customer doesn't have the time or inclination to do these things themselves, but they do have the money to pay you to do it for them.

When you inject calls-to-action and talk about your own services in your book, know who you're talking to. Know who will listen to you. Do not waste the time of a reader who is not your customer, and do not waste your own time trying to sell them something they will never buy.

To most readers, you are an expert giving out advice to help them do it themselves. But to the remaining 20 to 30%—your customers—you are their business partner that can do it for them.

WANT TO KNOW MORE?

Throughout the book, we have spoken briefly about calls-to-action, but not in much detail. Calls-to-action are the predominant method for generating leads. In a call-to-action, you are asking your reader to take some action that benefits both of you. You may ask them to take one of your courses or go to your website. You will then attempt to move them into your network, so that you can contact them later on when you have something valuable to offer them.

Essentially, you are transforming an interested reader into an invested customer. You can ask them directly to go to your website and book your services; or you can ask them to take a course that gives them more information and then to contact you, so you can do it for them if they want more help.

But you have to think carefully about who your customer is and about how to filter your readers. You don't want a bad customer or someone who will take up your time asking questions but never pay you any money for the answers.

Where should you put a call-to-action? In places in your book where you have created a need for the reader to take action. If you're talking about how Microsoft Word notoriously ruins the formatting of books, that is the perfect time to mention your proprietary software (EvolveBookPublisher) that can solve the problem. You are bringing a problem to the forefront, so you can solve it for the reader.

Additionally, your very last chapter should be a call-to-action that asks those who want help to get it. If you have a relevant course, direct them to it. If you have a website, give them the link. If you have a newsletter, ask them if they want to join the mailing list.

Ask them to do something, anything, so that they don't begin and end simply as "people who have bought your book".

There is a valuable opportunity, even if they don't want to be your customers, to add them to your growing database of people interested in what you have to say about your field of interest. When you launch a new product or service, or when you publish another book, you can ask them to purchase it.

Reviews

Getting reviews of your book is a very important step in your overall marketing plans. In fact, you should also plan to have ongoing strategies to get more reviews as time goes on.

It's important to note that not all book reviews are created equal, and there are essentially two types of reviews.

Public reviews are from everyday readers of your book on their chosen platform, such as Amazon, Barnes & Noble, and Goodreads.

The more online reviews you can attract and the more positive they are, the better the conversion rate of visitors to sales on your book listing.

This can be hugely beneficial to your book sales because it can play a role in exposure and the "Also Purchased" section of Amazon, the "Related Products" section, etc.

However, you don't have a lot of control over what reviewers say and how they say it, so it's important to keep an eye on your reviews and respond accordingly.

You can also approach the Top Amazon Reviewers for reviews, which is a great way to get a better quality one that has credibility.

Professional book reviews, on the other hand, are written by critics who work for well-known and respected magazines, newspapers, online publications, blogs, and online paid review sources.

Public reviews don't affect your "BSR" or sales ranking on Amazon , but professional reviews are displayed in the "Editorial Reviews" section of your Amazon page. While they are impressive and important to include, they don't impact your ranking on Amazon.

Some useful tips for reviews once you have them:

- Add excerpts from your best reviews to your book cover or front area of your interior.
- Include Nook Reviews on your author or book website.
- Make use of your book reviews on your social media sites.
- Include your book reviews in press releases.
- Try to use your book reviews to get more reviews.
- Add your reviews to your book metadata (the various fields you complete when publishing your book on publishing platforms like Amazon).

What About a Bad Review?

This happens to even the best books and sometimes makes no sense at all. But the important message is not to get emotional or angry about it and lash out in the form of feedback on the review itself. Take a calm, measured approach to any response to avoid stirring up the reviewer even more.

Even worse, you could have yourself a "stalker" who seems to think it's their mission to expose you. Eventually, if given no oxygen, a "stalker" will give up and move on.

Don't let a bad review take control over your life either. We have seen authors get upset and make rash business decisions over a bad review when it's just one person's opinion.

Amazon has a great review system and generally works well, but once a review is placed on your book, it's very hard to get it removed. If the review isn't suitable, you can report it to Amazon, but they rarely remove it. You can vote the review down by choosing other reviews as "helpful" and ask your followers to do the same. If you have enough 5-star reviews, then this can have the effect of moving a bad one off the front page.

CAN ALL MY FAMILY AND FRIENDS REVIEW MY BOOK?

The short answer is NO. Amazon has ways to work out who your friends and family are and use social media to find you out. Also, if reviews are done on the same IP address as the rest of the family, they will know very quickly that you are up to something.

Many online book websites are under close scrutiny about their reviews, and fake ones are high on their list of priorities. The reviews could be deleted, or your book could even be removed if they believe you had something to do with it. So, be careful and make sure your reviews are acquired within the rules.

Here are some of the rules Amazon has that you need to be aware of:

- You cannot offer anything in exchange for a review.
- You cannot review your own book, and family and friends cannot review your book.
- Customers in the same household may not post multiple reviews of the same product.
- If your book has only sold a few copies but receives many reviews, those reviews may be removed.
- Reviews must be respectful.
- The review cannot post promotional content.
- The reviewer must be a recent customer on Amazon.
- The reviewer does not necessarily have to purchase the book.

It's been said that one thousand 5-star reviews on Amazon will set you up for life. If you look at any great book, they usually have well over that.

Make sure you create a Goodreads account and try to encourage reviews there as well. Since Goodreads is owned by Amazon, it will also help your overall status online.

So, make a plan on how you will get reviews for your book right now.

SOCIAL MEDIA

Social media is not necessarily the best way to make money or get sales, but it is easily the best place to build your perfect audience and make them feel like a part of your community. There is nowhere that people will talk about you and your book more than social media—and that's exactly what you want. Sure, you can get reviews on Amazon, but there's no conversation or community in that.

Social media is so important in today's digital age that you just won't be taken seriously if you don't (at least) have a dedicated Facebook page. If you don't have a social media presence, it's synonymous with not having a real identity on the internet.

It wasn't always like that, of course. Before social media, the most effective way of creating a following online was building up a mailing list. This is still a popular and effective approach today, but the same glaring flaws remain:

- What if someone doesn't check their email regularly?
- What if your email ends up in their spam/junk folder?
- It's a one-way street; the email is being sent from you to them, but you often aren't expecting a reply back unless they have an issue. Their only method of interaction is opening the email and clicking on links. It's very difficult to tell how your audience feels about your email with just those interactions.
- It's a very isolated system. Your followers can't see or talk to each other, and they aren't really encouraged to share your emails with their friends. This makes it more difficult to achieve organic growth.

But, with the advent of social media, these problems have all but disappeared. Almost everyone who uses social media checks it multiple times a day; the system is designed to promote your posts to followers; there isn't a spam folder; and users have the option to "like", share, and comment. Random users may find your Facebook group just by searching for something like it and join up.

Friends of followers can see what they're doing and how they're interacting in your group, and your followers can easily grab their friends' attention by mentioning them. And more importantly, your followers can talk to each other! Your group can begin to take on a life of its own without you even realising it.

And the best part about social media is that your audience doesn't have to come to you; you're coming to them. It's much more convenient for them, and they're much more open to having your presence in their lives. They don't have to leave the comfort of Facebook, YouTube, or Instagram just to be a part of your community.

WHAT SOCIAL MEDIA PLATFORMS ARE THE BEST?

With the proliferation of social media sites, it's easy to be overwhelmed. Which ones are important, and which ones aren't? Which ones have the most reach? And do you really have to set up an account on all of them?

It's certainly true that not all social media platforms are created equal. The most important one is undoubtedly Facebook, which has almost 2 billion active users, and almost everyone you know has an account. It also has a lot more flexibility than other sites because it also caters to people using the site for business purposes. Create an account on Facebook and create a Facebook group based around your book. Ideally you should do this before you actually launch your book, so you can create a community beforehand.

The other crucial social sites are YouTube and Twitter. These are sites that you should absolutely create an account on, not just for marketing your book, but your business as well. If you don't already have an account for your business on these sites, you should create one now.

If you want to establish a very broad social media presence, these social sites are also great, depending on the content you're planning on posting:

- LinkedIn
- Instagram
- Goodreads
- Pinterest

After setting up an account on these social sites, you need to post regular content and build up a community. This is particularly crucial with Facebook and Twitter, but posting regular content on YouTube is not as necessary because it requires a lot more commitment.

Your strategy and the type of content you post will change from site to site, but you generally want to aim for regular content and high engagement.

This means getting readers to take action, and this mainly means commenting. Ask your readers, for example, what they're struggling with the most right now in their marketing. And respond to them when they comment! This is really important because they then feel more encouraged to make more comments, and you raise engagement. When other people see this, they also feel encouraged.

This is the power of social media.

How to Market Your Book on Social Media

Marketing your book on social media can be done in several similar ways. You can share the development of your book with the group by saying, "Right now, I'm writing a book about marketing. In it, I talk about how to improve your email marketing strategy. I talk about creating better headlines and repeating your call-to-action several times throughout the email. Have you been having email marketing problems? What are they? Share them in the comments".

You start by providing a brief description of part of your book, give readers something helpful to focus on, and finally ask them what problems they've been having. You provide some value first, and then you ask the reader to take action. It's a formula that you should follow for most of your posts.

Other times, you can be a bit more direct with your marketing and say, "My book was just released, and as part of a special promotion, it's only 99 cents to purchase right now! But the price will be going up next week, so if you want it, get it now."

Also, you should take the opportunity to film yourself saying the same kinds of things occasionally to add some variety and humanity to it. Particularly on Facebook. Pure text posts can be boring, so do some video and image-centric posts once in a while.

These strategies apply to both Facebook and Twitter, but YouTube is different. Because content takes longer to make, the runtime also tends to be longer.

Here are some ideas for videos you could film for your YouTube channel to promote your book:

- Film a short "trailer" for your book where you explain what it's about, who it's aimed at, why you wrote it, and who it can help. At the end, tell your viewers where they can purchase the book. This should be 2 to 5 minutes long. Try to keep it simple; imagine it as a conversation between you and the viewer. Don't go overboard with the editing.
- Take one chapter from your book and explain the content to the viewer. This serves as an extended teaser of the book, as proof that it has value to offer readers. This should be 3 to 5 minutes long.
- Take a question from your Facebook or Twitter account that somebody asked and answer it in the form of a short video. You could also take a question that clients ask you often and answer that.

The most important thing is that you position yourself as an expert; you are someone that people can except good and effective advice from. That is why you should be writing these posts and filming these videos.

When people see you as an expert, they'll think, "I want to know more. I should buy the book".

You don't have to advertise your book every day on social media to do this. Often, the best way is to let people convince themselves that they want to buy it.

But with that said, you should take advantage of your reach and mention promotions, discounts, and giveaways whenever they happen to remind people of your book's existence. You should also talk about topics that you cover in your book and direct people to it if they want to know more.

One last thing before you create social media accounts for your book: think about whether you will have multiple books in the future. The challenge is that some entrepreneurs will get carried away creating an account for every book they do. This means a lot of maintenance and separated followers, which means lower engagement overall.

Often an author will get so excited about their new book, they want to "give it a home" without thinking out their social media strategy first.

We recommend that you:

- Create a Facebook Author Page (and other platforms as applicable).
- Consider if you need social media accounts specific to your book or whether people can simply follow you personally.
- If you feel you need a business name or brand, then try to focus on that as your core social media account, and use your book to compliment that brand inside your account rather than separating your business and your book into their own individual identities.

Author Website

One of the most important things you can do for your book (and for your future books) is building your author website—the right way.

When readers finish your book and want more, your author website presents a golden opportunity to convert them into a follower. While you can do this using Twitter, Facebook, or Instagram, these are best used in conjunction with your author website, not as a replacement. An author website has the power to be an all-in-one place where your followers can learn everything about you, buy anything from you, and easily refer their friends to you. If done correctly, it's a lot more organised and centralised than a Facebook or Instagram page will ever be, with no character limit on what you want to convey to your audience as in the case of Twitter.

These are things that an author website has and can do that social media simply can't replicate:

- Offer all of your books in all formats, purchased directly from you, the author, as well as a list of all the sites where your book is sold (with any affiliate codes built-in)

- Offer links to and information about all of the products and services that your business offers
- Allow a dedicated space for all of your testimonials
- Offer space for your blog, which furthers the content of your book and retains the interest of your followers
- Provide links to all of your social media pages

Social media is not a substitution for your author website, and it doesn't work the other way around either. Your author website is the hub from which your followers—your readers—can glean everything about you and everything you're saying. You should be able to access all of your social media, your blog, and anything else relevant to your readership from the same site. It's a way of bringing everything together.

Here is an example of an author website that utilises these benefits: www.johnnorth.com.au.

You should always try to secure a website in your own name.

Author Website Secrets to Success

However, there are a number of pitfalls you can fall into when building your author website. These are the most important secrets to remember:

Secret #1 — Design Your Website to Sell

It's common to focus on the design of the website, without focusing all that much on the design of the content. Content design problems include: the "About the Author" section is 1,000 words long, the "Books" page has a single direct link and only includes the latest book, there is a single link to an inactive Facebook page and no presence on social media otherwise. The focus is placed in all the wrong areas.

Your "About" section should be informative, but try to keep it to less than 250 words because no one wants to read that much about you unless you're already a celebrity. Your "Books" page should include all your books and links to the most popular sites your book is being sold from. Not everyone wants to buy directly from you, possibly because they're more familiar with Amazon or Book Depository. And you should have a social media presence to the point that you post regularly.

Designing your website to sell doesn't just mean getting people to buy your book. Often readers who have already finished your book go to your author page to see what else you've done. Your author website is meant to sell YOU to your readers. You should be focused on converting them to followers. If they end up buying another book, great. But you want them to hang around. And one of the best ways to do that is ... a blog.

How To Stick To Your Goal

👤 John North 📅 Feb 4, 2019 🏷 Blog

Setting goals are the first step your "living the dream". It is vital to achieving what you have always desired to have or desired to be. Although setting goals to help paint a clearer picture of your future, it only keeps you motivated for so long. You may get bored after some time, and eventually completely lose your way around. If you want to be successful, that is something you should avoid. Here are a few tips so you won't steer away from the goals you've always wanted to pursue.

Read more ❯

4 Reasons to Create Your Own Podcast for Your Business or Hobby

👤 John North 📅 Jan 30, 2019 🏷 Blog

Podcasting is a powerful, inexpensive and easy new medium for sharing your message with a focused and passionate audience. As a podcaster you'll become a recognized expert in your area of interest or expertise.

Read more ❯

Holding Yourself Accountable In Making Your Goals Happen

👤 John North 📅 Dec 23, 2018 🏷 Blog

3 Books To Read For Ultimate Motivation

👤 John North 📅 Dec 6, 2018 🏷 Blog

SECRET #2 —CREATE A BLOG

If at all possible, you should create a blog on your author website (that is regularly updated), so you can retain readership. Take them from being followers of your books to followers of you. A blog is a great way to do that because you're always posting new content that encourage your readership to come back to your website. You can use your blog to announce a new book, a new product or service, or an upcoming event. You can give advice in a blog and advertise your services at the bottom.

Blogs are the easiest and most consistent way to retain regular viewership on your website, and it's an easy way to announce something new to the most dedicated portion of your followers. Otherwise, what will keep your audience coming back if nothing new is happening every week?

SECRET #3—TAKE INSPIRATION, BUT DON'T IMITATE

The design of your website isn't the most important thing about your website, but it is important. But you may not know where to start. There are tens of thousands of author websites out there, so you have a lot of sites to take inspiration from. You should not, however, copy the design of another website wholesale. If your website looks like every other author website, readers will instantly recoil upon seeing it. They won't want to look at the content because they'll be too focused on the same design they've seen a hundred times before.

The secret here is to take inspiration from sites you really like without stealing everything. A great strategy, in fact, is to take parts from one website and other parts from another website that fit well together.

NEED HELP CREATING YOUR AUTHOR WEBSITE?

Creating your author website is important, but it can also be very time-consuming, and it can take several months to even get it operational. The Evolvepreneur Platform was designed to greatly simplify and expedite the process. If you want to find out more, go to:

HTTPS://EVOLVEPRENEUR.APP/

Websites vs. Funnels

You might be asking why we're even talking about websites or funnels. After all, isn't this a book about writing a book?

One of the biggest challenges we see is that when an entrepreneur writes a book, spends months on it, and finally publishes and launches it ...

Then ... crickets!

No-one knows about it, so no-one buys it, and so no-one reads it, and so no-one talks about it.

Why? Because they never considered how they would sell and promote their book. They thought if they just focused on making something great, people would naturally flock to it. But even though just having your name as an author on Amazon will certainly drive traffic to your book by default, you need to also invest in an ongoing strategy to promote it.

Naturally, you may think to yourself, "I need a website." While an author-oriented website is a good idea because it helps to create credibility, it is unlikely to generate a reasonable number of sales purely from a credibility site. The era of the traditional website is coming to a close.

Why?

Like anything in this fast-moving world, saving time has become more important than ever. Website visitors are looking for quick answers to their questions. Most websites are used in the same way as brochures; they record prospects spending very little time on the site before bouncing out again.

These are some key reasons why your website is probably losing conversions and sales:

- A website isn't conversion-focused.
- A website simply has too many calls-to-action.

- The majority of content and offers on a website are untrackable.
- Websites are too hard to change if you're not a designer.
- A website can't easily help build a list of prospects.

Enter the Funnel ...

The "sales funnel" is a single-purpose page designed to get the visitor to do one thing, and one thing only. It is focused on conversion rates and fine-tuning sign-up rates, as well as conversion to a customer (meaning converting a visitor to the webpage into your customer).

We would have built hundreds of websites over the years, but most of them never made any money; none of them ever broke even on the cost of maintaining them. Once we started doing sales funnels, it narrowed our focus to just getting results. Not worrying about building a beautiful site or trying to cover every possibility means we had to get the message right.

We highly recommend that you look at a product we fell in love with called *Clickfunnels*. It changed our business, and, in the past three years, a single page has generated around a million dollars.

Check it out here: http://evlink.info/clickfunnels14daytrial

One of the greatest benefits of a funnel is that you can easily offer "upsells". McDonald's makes over a billion dollars in extra sales every year when they ask, "Would you like fries with that?"

So, for example, you could offer an eBook at a reasonably low price and then upsell to something more substantial, like a paperback version, complimentary behind-the-scenes videos on writing the book, or more detailed concepts not covered in the book.

Make sure all of your upsell strategies are, in fact, "good" for your customers, and you'll achieve great success in your upselling efforts.

Remember that upsells are simply math. Many find that 33% of their buyers will invest in something else in their catalog if given the opportunity. Provide your customers with the opportunity to spend more money with you.

Here are the models and options for upselling strategies:

Additional Products—if you have other products in your inventory and they match with the audience for your existing product, you should always consider selling them to your existing customers. They have already stated their intent to buy—you just need to give them more options.

Continuity Program—this is continuing content without one-on-one interaction. A continuity program is where members pay you on a recurring basis for access to you and/or perhaps an online course. The more people you get into your continuity program, the more money you make on the initial sale.

Coaching Program—continuing content with one-on-one interaction. You can charge a lot more for this—but understand that this isn't nearly as scalable.

Events—single big productions with a high-perceived value. You can sell the recording from your event for an additional revenue stream.

Software and/or Services—if the match is clear, a software program or service can be a great upsell strategy to implement. There is the obvious investment in the creation and maintenance of the program, but once it's completed, the revenue opportunities are considerable. If you can provide your software as a "software as a service" (SaaS) platform, you can continue to charge for access and it becomes another form of a continuity program.

We have developed a sales funnel around our own Evolvepreneur.club software platform. You can look at and analyse our funnel by going to https://evolvepreneur.biz/ freebooks and following the steps.

CREATING A
MARKETING PLAN

The work you put in before your book launch determines the success of your book. If you leave it for launch day, you may be left wondering why the hundreds of sales you were expecting didn't happen.

Writing a great book to widen your reach is a good start, but it's not enough. You need to promote it as well. That means a marketing plan. There are two main components to any marketing plan: **strategic marketing** and **tactical marketing**. You should create a marketing plan for your book. But before you start on this important task, it's vital you understand the difference between the two terms.

Strategic marketing is the content of your message. It's what you say and how you say it, including the concepts that you choose to focus on, the words and images you use to communicate those concepts, and the tone in which the message is delivered.

Tactical marketing, on the other hand, has to do with the execution of strategic marketing. For example, placing ads, building a website, attending trade shows, and things like that. If we ask a business owner about their marketing plan, the answer almost always comes back in terms of tactical marketing: they send direct mail, run radio ads, host a website, those sort of things.

The key to creating effective marketing is to master the strategic side. NOT the tactical.

What you say in your marketing and how you say it are almost always far more important than the marketing medium where you say it. Both are important, of course, but the real leverage is in the messaging itself. And that's the strategic side of marketing.

In fact, when a marketing campaign bombs, the tendency is almost always to blame the marketing medium, like the TV or radio station, which is the tactical part of the plan, without any regard to how good or bad the strategy behind that marketing piece was.

DEVELOPING YOUR BOOK MARKETING PLAN

You need to define the market that your book will be directed at. Get onto Facebook, Amazon, or Goodreads, and look at who is reading the type of book you plan to write.

Some questions to ask:

- Why do these potential customers buy this type of book?
- When do they buy them?
- How much would they be prepared to pay for your knowledge?

Consider your audience demographic characteristics for a minute:

- What is the prominent cultural, ethnic, religious, and racial background of your target book buying customers?
- What is the social class of your customers?
- How does your target market break down by gender?
- What are their occupations?
- Who makes the buying decision?
- What are the wants and needs of your target market?
- What are the key traits of your product or service?
- What is the size of the market?

Here are a few key action steps in your book marketing plan:

- Create a list of everyone you know that could buy your book.
- Plan to get reviews for your book.
- Create a video book trailer for your book.
- Try to get interviews for your book when it is released.

Our EvolveInstantAuthor.com course includes a template for a book marketing plan that you can use as a basis for developing one of your own.

STEP 5:
EVOLVING
YOUR BOOK

One of the most common questions we get asked by authors is: "What's next?"

Writing your book is the beginning, not the end. It's the start of your journey as an author to convince your audience about your credibility and what you offer.

Your book is one of the foundations for your business. Once it's published, there are numerous ways to leverage it.

A lot of authors will think that once they have published their book, they can relax, forget about it, and move onto the next project on their "to-do" list.

But now is the time to get moving!

You need to promote the book until you are sick of hearing about it. At that point, you may think that you have done enough, but the reality is that virtually no one knows about it.

In this stage, we will cover:

- Going from being an author to being an authority
- How to expand from your book
- The bookselling system
- "Dream Sell 100"

This stage is about revealing the secrets to the next stage of your book journey. This is where the real money is made, and more often than not, it is criminally overlooked and under-appreciated by most authors.

Becoming An Authority

Did you know that "author" is short for "author-ity"?

The Huffington Post says: *"That 'authority' and 'author' share the same root is a given in publishing circles. To become an author you should have authority in your subject, and those with authority often write books. The trajectory of authorship goes like this: You work to become an expert on a particular topic. You author articles and books. The more you publish, the more you embody the very definition of authority: 'the confident quality of someone who knows a lot about something' ."*

The general public will perceive you as an expert or authority on your chosen subject based simply on the evidence of your written book. Now is the time to reinforce your authority in the marketplace. You want to strategically place yourself in the public eye. For example:

- Writing press releases about your book
- Booking podcast interviews
- Broadcasting Facebook Lives
- Participating in radio interviews
- Making TV appearances
- Posting blog articles

Some assets you need to create:

- One- and two-page BIO and media sheet
- Great BIO that is broken into a very short version and longer versions, depending on the time you have with the interviewer
- A bunch of "sound bytes" about you and your book that you can use when the time is short (e.g.. a three-minute TV interview)

- Short book summary
- Book images that look like they are in 3Dor that feature your book in different places

We have created media sheets for several of our clients. Here is a couple to look at for ideas:

- https://genuinely-you.co and choose "Work with Gina".
- https://drwarrickbishop.com choose "Media".

Make sure you keep good records of all your media appearances, including screenshots, website addresses, and any other relevant information. You will see on the above sites that we create a blog and have a specific category, so we can keep a track of these authors' appearances.

If you do live appearances or speeches, make sure you take good quality photos or even video of the presentation. It's common for us to ask an author about their previous work only to be told that they never took any photos!

Also consider running a "social proof campaign" where you ask your current customers to create videos, audios, or written testimonials.

Here is a sample of what we ask our clients that participate in our "social proof campaigns":

- What's your name and what do you do?
- What was life like before Evolvepreneur Marketing Services, including the biggest challenge you were having?
- What is life like now after Evolvepreneur Marketing Services, including the single biggest benefit, breakthrough, or positive change?
- Can you say a few final words of thanks for Evolvepreneur Marketing Services?

Expanding from the Book

You may think the book is the endpoint. But a book just starts you on your journey, and you need to consider what is next on your list.

For example, your book could be:

- Turned into a course
- Used to create a membership program or mastermind group
- Used to create an audiobook
- Leveraged to create a community or movement

At the same time, consider putting a book review strategy in place. Asking for 5-star reviews in a constant and formal way is a great way to grow your authority on Amazon. It's been said (once already in this very book!) that if you have a 1,000 reviews on Amazon, you are set for life. Of course, that doesn't mean one-star reviews!

You need to view your book as a 24/7 asset, working away constantly to drive business your way. But this takes work. The idea, "Build it and they will come", will not work on Amazon when you are up against 3 million other books.

Your role now is to get your message seen and heard in as many places as you can. So, making sure that your book is published on all the platforms possible is an important start. Don't forget Apple iBooks, Kobo, Barnes & Noble, and Google Books.

Here are some ideas to expand your book further:

- Bundle books into a speaker engagement fee and allow the hosting party to sell the books for you at the event.
- Offer to appear on TV to talk about your new book.

- Offer to write articles for the local newspaper or magazine about your ideas from your book.
- Run Amazon ads to drive consistent book sales.
- Create a Facebook or LinkedIn group around your book to expand your community.
- Giveaway the first 3 chapters of your book to lead into upselling the whole book.
- Create your own online TV show around your book using Facebook Live or Youtube Live.
- Offer to do book signings at local bookstores if they will stock your book.
- Run Facebook or Google ads to drive traffic to your book sales pages.
- Run webinars to help explain your book ideas.
- Have local meetups to build a community around your book; take a look at meetup.com.

There are many ways to get your book to the market place, but not all of them will work. It's important to test and measure strategies until you find the 2 or 3 that work the best. Don't just settle for one way because that might stop working, leaving you struggling to find alternatives.

You need to be always looking for ways to expand your book into different formats because it will also help your authority in the marketplace. The more "variations", the more potential traffic to your website or buyers for the book.

THE BOOK-SELLING SYSTEM

You need to design your own personal "book-selling system", which complements and promotes your book to drive prospects to you. Some components of this type of system include:

- Branded images and content that attracts your prospect's attention
- Book funnels to convert traffic to take action
- Author Authority Website
- Free bonuses (cheat sheets, checklists)
- Upsells when people buy your book (e.g., audiobook, video, or processes)

Make a decision on how you will fulfill the orders if you are going with physical books. Consider how this will be done. If digital, make sure the files are easily accessible and perhaps protected from copying as well.

Think about how to add value to your book so that the reader will continue their journey and experience with you.

Based on what we have talked about in this final stage, you need to write down a simple plan to make sure you have several ideas in progress to start to making sales of your book.

A few pitfalls we see:

- Don't buy thousands of physical books unless you know you can sell them! You can always buy smaller quantities from on-demand platforms such as Amazon.
- Try testing your ideas on digital books first before you get into physical copies.
- Don't over-complicate your funnels to start with; start simple and test your market.
- Be prepared to fail. In fact, expect it. Sometimes the ugly promotions work better than the slick ones!

You need a consistent and cost-effective plan that will sustain your book marketing for the long term. Spend some time working out your plan and start taking small action steps to gain some initial momentum.

Here is a great idea to promote your book when you don't have enough physical copies to go around: we have created a light cardboard handout with a perforated cut line (see image below). Basically, it gives the reader a bookmark and a promotional tear-off for their friend. It is great way to promote your book at low cost and even to add value with its complimentary bookmark.

Here is an example one of ours:

The "Dream Sell 100"

In this chapter, we outline a strategy we call the "Dream Sell 100", and it's an important concept to consider.

Here is how the "Dream Sell 100" works.

First, remember the old 80/20 rule: twenty percent of buyers will bring you 80% of your revenue. Accordingly, focusing on the 20% will always bring you a greater impact, and it's also much more cost effective.

If you're spending $1,000 a month on advertising, you're probably using a "shotgun" approach to a broad market, 99.9% of whom will never buy what you have to offer.

What if you could take that same $1,000 a month and target the top one hundred prospects, aka your "dream sell 100" prospects, in your area or niche?

To do so, you'd have to have your business go through the following progression in the minds of your market's best potential buyers:

- *I've never heard of that business.*
- *I think I've heard of that business.*
- *Oh yeah, I've heard of that business.*
- *I want to know more about that business.*
- *I like that business!*
- *That's the business that I work with.*
- *You have got to check out this business!*

This is what Malcolm Gladwell talks about in *The Tipping Point*, which is about bringing your business to the place where it's the talk of the community and your popularity is unstoppable.

Your top one hundred prospects might be only 25 people, or it might be 250, but it's always cheaper to go after the best and most influential buyers, rather than all buyers.

Let's say you send your "Dream Sell 100" prospects a personal letter or email. Your target group will now hear from you once a month—at a minimum. Most of the people on the list will probably ignore your approach the first four or five times they get it, but remember that you're committed to building a reputation, not simply getting clients.

Building a reputation is a strategic objective, not solely tactical. And if you want to build one on purpose, this means that you must be targeting the people who will help you accomplish this faster.

And who are they?

Your best buyers. Your "dream sell 100" most ideal clients.

You're going to get something out to these people every month, even if it's only a letter or flyer. It won't cost you a lot of money. Just the price of a stamp and an envelope (and maybe an attention grabber), but it will be very effective.

The first thing you're going to do is send them a letter introducing yourself and offer them something free. Then you're going to continue to contact them every month. You use that opportunity not just to sell but to show that you're the industry authority.

That means you use education-based marketing—telling them what's happening in your industry, what to look for, what to avoid ... and why you're the most logical choice when they decide to buy.

Consider that one of the top one hundred just might become your customer for life ... and how that would change everything for you. Keep up the mailing campaign, and you may land several new customers over the year. The key is always repetition.

You could implement this strategy to get reviews for your book or use it to sell your book. You could even use your book to leverage a meeting. For example, you could gift a book on

Amazon, and they will wrap it and deliver it to your prospect. This could make a big impression on this ideal potential customer so that they become your customer for life.

Ask yourself now if you could implement this strategy for your book.

WHERE TO FROM HERE?

START TODAY!

We have reached the end of this book. We have covered a lot of content and secrets to publishing. It represents hundreds of hours we have spent helping entrepreneurs to become published authors.

It's time for you to take the next steps towards your own publishing journey. Don't just read this book and decide that one day you will make a start. The best way to get started is to complete some small action steps to gain momentum and confidence that you can actually do this, for instance:

1. Think of some titles and subtitles, and ask your associates what they think of them. Tell them you are writing a book and need their input.
2. Write up a brief summary of what your book could be about and put the same idea to your associates.
3. Write up a potential table of contents of your new book.

This should only take you 1 to 2 hours at most.

We have given you the necessary steps throughout the book to create, complete, promote, and evolve your book. Make sure you visit www.evolveinstantauthor.com, and get your "book plan" to help you with the correct steps in the ideal sequence.

The reality is that by breaking this project into small chunks, you will achieve a massive result if you continue the work over time. This could be simply an hour or so a week, or a dedicated hour every day for a month.

Tell people you want to write a book. Once you tell the world, it makes it much harder for you to put it off.

Do whatever you can to make yourself accountable to achieve this result. This will be the best action you will ever undertake.

If you feel you need help to get this project done—and more often than not, it can be a big task for anyone who is very busy or really isn't technically able to do the whole process—reach out to us via www.evolveglobalpublishing.com or grab our online course at www.evolveinstantauthor.com.

If you loved this book, we would be honored by a 5-star review on the platform you bought this copy.

One last thing: please join our free Facebook group, which is available from https://www.facebook.com/groups/evolvebooklaunchteam, and let us know how you are going.

Start right now.

Do one small task.

We look forward to hearing from you soon!

OTHER BOOKS

THE 5 STAGES TO ENTREPRENEURIAL SUCCESS

#1 BEST SELLER

What Every Entrepreneur Should Know About **DOMINATING YOUR MARKET**

JOHN NORTH

The 5 Stages To Entrepreneurial Success:

It's a common question, but what makes a successful entrepreneur?

It's my belief that success isn't just about making money. Most people start a business for the freedom they expect it to give them. The cold hard reality is that most entrepreneurs end up working longer hours and for a lot less than a typical wage for an average job.

Entrepreneurs commit to "the hustle" because they have a much bigger vision for their future than the average person. But then, if they work harder than an average worker, then why doesn't every entrepreneur become massively successful?

The fact is, many entrepreneurs are making the same mistakes year after year. Learn what those are and how to avoid them in **The 5 Stages To Entrepreneurial Success.**

https://evolvepreneur.club/show-book/B072N3XWXY

EVERYTHING You Know About MARKETING IS WRONG!

How to Immediately Generate More Leads, Attract More Clients and Make More Money

JOHN NORTH

Everything You Know About Marketing Is Wrong!

In this #1 Best Selling Book, we'll reveal the strategies you can immediately deploy that will enable you to out-think, out-market and out-sell your competition.

What we want to do in this book is to teach you a system for marketing your business... to a point where it becomes instantly obvious to your prospects that they would be an idiot to do business with anyone other than you... at any time, anywhere or at any price.

What most business owners will focus on is generating more leads at any cost but this isn't the best way to attract prospects to your business.

We can help you build a million-dollar or even multi-million-dollar business. Also, make sure you take advantage of the free bonuses in the book!

https://evolvepreneur.club/show-book/B00RMF0E4I

OTHER BOOKS

THE SECRET PUBLISHING KIT

Go to www.evolveglobalpublishing.com/spk to get free instant access to our special book bonus.

Your "Secret Publishing Kit" includes:

- Checklists for the 90-Day Book Publishing Plan
- Publishing Cheat Sheets
- Sample Book Marketing Plan
- Sample Marketing Images
- Promotional Marketing Ideas
- Sample Media Kit
- Special "Would You Like to Create a Quality Book That Attracts Clients Like Crazy?" Report

CPSIA information can be obtained
at www.ICGtesting.com
Printed in the USA
BVHW081023220419
546159BV00027B/1922/P